UP AGAINST IT

DUE

to Art and Eva

UP AGAINST

 **IT** Children
and the
law in
Canada

JEFFERY WILSON

ANANSI 🔘   **TORONTO**

Published with the assistance of the Canada Council and the Ontario
Arts Council.

Cover design: Joss Maclennan
Author photograph: Steven Wilson
Typesetting: Imprint Typesetting
Made in Canada by The Hunter Rose Company
for the
House of Anansi Press Limited
35 Britain Street
Toronto, Ontario   M5A 1R7
80 81 82 83 84 85 86   5 4 3 2 1

Canadian Cataloguing in Publication Data
Wilson, Jeffery.
   Up against it
ISBN 0-88784-076-0 pa.
1. Children — Law — Canada. I. Title.
KE512.W542   346'.71'013   C79-094058-2

TABLE OF CONTENTS

PREFACE

The 1970's saw some worthy attempts to explore the condition of children in Canada, culminating in the splash of media events for the International Year of the Child. On paper, our children have never had so much attention from so many. Books and articles abounded. One Toronto programme took three years, a million dollars and an impressive mix of professionals from psychiatry, law, urban geography, sociology, psychology and anthropology. Much was discussed. In 1975, a British Columbia Royal Commission chaired by Justice Thomas R. Berger drew up a charter of children's rights, along with suggestions for implementation. The report, a model of its kind, may now be found gathering dust in law libraries across Canada. It seems that nothing is too good for our children, as long as we don't have to go beyond talk.

Do we need more than talk? Surely even the most casual newspaper reader must be aware that all is not well with the children in our society. Our image of a Canadian childhood may be based on the rural paradises of *Ann of Green Gables* or *Who Has Seen the Wind*, but the modern reality more likely includes the shopping mall, the street corner, the teenaged drug abuser, the child suicide, the AWOL kid struggling in our cities to find a job, a fake I.D., a warm place to sleep for the night. Fewer families today bother to stay together even "for the sake of the children", and an alarming number of children are experts in the ways of custody, child support, divorce settlements and child welfare. The rate of crimes committed by and against children rises inexorably, and is a national disgrace.

Our laws must deal with these contemporary children, as well as children who are the victims of antiquated school systems, stingy rehabilitation programmes, economic disasters or plain bad luck. We should know better, but still we flunk the child with special needs and disabilities, and then brand him as a juvenile delinquent when he skips school in boredom to rip off a candy store. We wrench the Native child from his environment and are shocked when he does not immediately "adjust" and thank us for it. The days of *Oliver Twist*, with its workhouses and child pickpockets, may be over, but in some ways our age is even more horrifying: the age of *Clockwork Orange*, say, with many children in a direct collision course with their own hostile and indifferent society, the age of punk rock, unemployment, and eleven-year-old alcoholics.

Canadian children's law has a good reputation abroad for being flexible and efficient, but from the child's point of view, our legal system leaves much to be desired. In the following pages, I've tried to shed some light on the struggles of our children within the system, while providing a practical guide to the law for parents, social workers, teachers, or anybody who is involved with children. I hope the book will contribute, however modestly, to the kind of activism in child advocacy which is now necessary and will be all the more essential in this decade. We need to revise our thinking about children; we need to see them as living citizens with rights and feelings, not pawns in a sociological game.

For clarity's sake, I've had to simplify many complex issues and have ignored some areas altogether, such as immigration law. For those who want more specialized detail, there is a short reading list at the back; many of my Provincial examples come from Ontario, since that's my home base, and I can only hope that readers in other Provinces will check out variations in their local parliaments. UP AGAINST IT is not meant to be the last word, only the beginnings of a basic grammar. For their patient aid in putting it together, I'd like to thank the people at Anansi Press: Jim Polk, Ann Wall, and Sally Cohen. The assistance of Betty Krieger with the manuscript drafts is gratefully acknowledged. Once again, I thank my friend Mary Tomlinson, who edited the early drafts, and without whose help, I am sure, this book would not have been possible.

—Jeffery Wilson Toronto

1

THE CHILD AS VICTIM
THE CHILD AS CRIMINAL

In our society it has long been acceptable to hit children. Spare the rod and spoil the child; "A good spanking", even "a good beating", can be sanctioned in the name of discipline or care; folk wisdom agrees that unruly kids need to be "slapped into line" from time to time. The law reflects this belief, as we find in Section 43 of the *Criminal Code:*

> Every school teacher, parent or person standing in the place of the parent is justified in using force by way of correction toward a pupil or child, as the case may be, who is under his care, if the force does not exceed what is reasonable under the circumstances.

Such "correction" seems to run against the grain of our society's general rules against assault, and many parents find this Section controversial. It is argued that this sanction of "discipline" invites parents to punish their children beyond reasonable limits, and the nature of those limits provokes much discussion.

Few politicians in Canada would dare to legislate a spanking out of existence, as Sweden has recently done; it may be that such a law would not be acceptable to most Canadian parents, and would be next to impossible to enforce. Yet one man's "discipline" may be another man's "physical abuse", and the *Criminal Code* and the *Child Welfare Act* have several provisions which attempt to detail the kind of care and protection our society expects of a child's custodian. To read through some of these provisions is to remind ourselves that children are the most vulnerable of all our "minority groups": the terror some of them must undergo almost defies belief.

Assault causing bodily harm—S. 255 (2) of The Criminal Code: This Section was applicable in the case of a mother and father who inflicted third-degree burns as a form of punishment upon their three-year old child, cruelly neglecting to have the wounds medically treated. The court in the first instance sentenced the accused mother and father to two years imprisonment in light of the parents' limited emotional and mental capacity. On appeal, this sentence was increased to five years, the Appellate Court rejecting the notion that the parents were unable to understand the severity of their actions. It found that the public interest must be protected through the deterrent value of a heavy penalty.

Abuse and Reporting Provisions: S. 47 of The Child Welfare Act, 1978 defines "abuse" as a condition of physical harm, malnutrition or mental illness, that, if not remedied, could seriously impair growth, development or result in permanent injury; or the fact of a child being sexually molested. Section 49 of the same Act requires every person who has information of the abandonment, desertion or need for protection of a child, or the infliction of abuse upon a child, to immediately report the information to a Children's Aid Society. This requirement applies to all professionals, whether or not the information is "confidential" in nature involving a therapist, the family doctor, a priest, a teacher, welfare officer, tax investigator, or politician.

The only exception is information told to a lawyer, who, acting as the person's solicitor, receives information from that client concerning the abuse of a child. For example, say a lawyer is retained by a parent to prevent his child from being removed from the home due to allegations of child abuse. During one of the interviews, the client indicates that he did inflict punishment on the child by way of a strap resulting in welts and lacerations to the child's body. The lawyer may or may not refer his client to an agency to remedy this abusive form of parenting, but he is under no duty to report this information to the authorities. However, if a person who happens to be a lawyer receives information from someone other than a client concerning the abuse of a child, there is no exception to the reporting rule.

The Act protects the professional by disallowing law suits against them for reporting, and conversely it imposes a fine of up to $1,000 against that professional for failure to report. In fact, the person who fails to report is theoretically liable under S. 423 (2) (a) of the *Criminal Code* which makes it an indictable offence to conspire to effect an unlawful purpose, in this case, failure to report abuse. This Section would apply to a doctor who might comply with parental wishes not to report the apparent abuse of their child.

Morever, there is the possibility that failing to report abuse renders an individual, and particularly the professional, negligent in exercising his duty. In one California case, a physician and a hospital were found liable for injuries sustained by a child when the doctor, in the employ of the hospital, failed without valid reason to diagnose and report "battered child syndrome", the effect of which was that the child was returned to his parents, receiving further injuries. The court held that an awareness of the "battered child syndrome" and its effects on a child's welfare was knowledge and skill which is ordinarily possessed and exercised by the medical profession, and therefore failure to report same is a breach of a doctor's standard of care or duty.

To insure that repeated incidents of abuse do not go unnoticed, the *Child Welfare Act, 1978* creates the label of "registered person" which means a person named in or otherwise identifiable from a Register created for the purpose of recording information received by Children's Aid Societies concerning abuse of children. It should be noted that the names of those persons who report incidents of abuse or neglect (in other words, the "informant") will not be disclosed to the court, or to the public, nor will it be recorded in the Register. The information in the Register will be made available to a Coroner, a legally qualified medical practitioner, or police officer duly authorized for the purpose of a Coroner's investigation. It is also open to the Official Guardian or his agent to assist him in commencing an action to recover damages for any injuries caused to a child as a result of the abuse. Further to this, the information is to be made available to the Director of the Registry, and various other designated persons.

When an entry is made in the Register, the Director must notify in writing the registered person who is alleged or suspected to have inflicted abuse upon a child, informing him that:

(a) his name has been recorded in the Register or that he is otherwise identifiable from the Register;

(b) he is entitled to inspect the information in the Register that refers to or identifies himself; and

(c) he is entitled to request the Director to expunge his name from the Register or to have it otherwise amended.

The Act establishes a hearing procedure for that person who makes such a request and is denied, and provides for the right to appeal to Ontario's Divisional Court from the tribunal decision.

Other Offences: The Criminal Code

Incest — S. 150: Incest is a criminal offence which is committed when a person, knowing that another person is his parent, child, brother, sister, grandparent, or grandchild, has sexual intercourse with him or her. "Brother" and "sister" include a half brother and half sister.

Seduction — S. 151: This offence occurs when a male person of eighteen years of age or more, seduces a female person of an obviously chaste character, who is sixteen to eighteen years of age. The word "seduces" refers to the use of persuasion, solicitation, promises, bribes, or other means without the use of force for the purpose of achieving a consent from the woman. In this respect, a "seduction" is to be distinguished from a "rape".

Illicit Sexual Intercourse — S. 153: This is an offence for the action of any male person who has sexual intercourse with his step-daughter, foster daughter, or female ward. The fact that the daughter has consented is no defence to the action.

Procurement and Sexual Immorality — Ss. 166 and 168: Procurement refers to any parent or guardian of a female child who permits or encourages the child to have sexual intercourse with a person and to receive payment for that act. Sexual immorality refers to a condition in the home of a child where persons are participating in adultery or unacceptable conduct which might endanger the moral welfare of the child.

Neglecting to Obtain Assistance in Childbirth — S. 226: This Section holds a woman to be guilty of an offence and liable to imprisonment if she, being pregnant, intentionally interferes with the child's life or conceals the birth, failing to make provision for reasonable assistance in respect of her delivery. The Section is applicable if the child is permanently injured or dies immediately before, during or in a short time after birth. The provision focuses upon the protection of children surrounding the event of delivery. For example, when, as a result of a mother's actions, a child who was born at 9 o'clock in the morning, dies at 5 o'clock in the afternoon, this Section would not be applicable because death did not occur a short time after birth. One must then utilize the infanticide Section of the *Criminal Code.*

Infanticide — S. 216: Unless the mother can show that she has not fully recovered from the effects of giving birth to the child, including the effects of lactation, such that her mind was "disturbed" she will be liable to the offence of infanticide when, by her wilful act or omission, she causes the death of a newborn child. "Newly born child" refers to persons under the age of one year. After that age, an accused would be subject to a charge of murder or manslaughter.

Neglect — S. 197: Every person who is a parent, foster parent, guardian or head of a family, is responsible for providing necessaries of life for their child under the age of sixteen years. Under this Section, evidence that a person has in any way recognized a child as being his own is, in the absence of any evidence to the contrary, proof that the child is his child. That is, this Section is not restricted to a biological definition of "child". This reflects society's recognition that children, here defined as persons under the age of sixteen years, do not have the physical or economic ability to provide for themselves. Accordingly, not only do we consider there to be a civil obligation upon a parent to provide support for a child, but we invoke the criminal law and its severe sanctions to ensure that children are economically protected. If neglect leads to bodily harm or death, the parent can possibly face criminal charges. Consider the case of the Christian Scientist who followed his belief in refusing to provide needed medical treatment for his child, who died as a result. The Ontario Court of Appeal in 1903 stated:

> It is shocking if in the case of infants they . . . were to be exposed to danger from contagious or infectious diseases which the instructive common sense of mankind in general does not as yet find or admit to be curable by means only of subjective or mental treatment.[1]

Abandonment — S. 200: Leaving a child under the age of ten years and thereby endangering his health or life makes one liable to an indictable offence and possible imprisonment for two years.

Causing a Child to Beg or Perform — S. 53: Child Welfare Act, 1978: A person cannot cause or make a financial arrangement which results in a child being in a public place for the purpose of begging or receiving charity or for the purpose of singing, playing, or performing, or making any money. Children can perform in a circus, theatre, or, as the Act says, a "place of public amusement" only on the express permission of the head of the City Council where the entertainment is to take place. This Section is designed to ensure that children will not be exploited and will be treated properly when they are performing or entertaining, but the frequency of the invocation is probably quite minimal.

In one case, I spent several months trying to locate enforcement personnel in Toronto and was passed from the Mayor to the Chairman of the Municipality, both offices of which disclaimed any knowledge of this Section and referred me to the local Children's Aid Society, who referred me back to the office of the Mayor or the Chairman. Eventually, I gave up and the child is currently entertaining for the purpose of profit, as yet with no detrimental affects. Does this Section apply to the hundreds of "cute" children who appear on TV on behalf of McDonald's, Kellogg's corn flakes, Century 21, and the like? Apparently, the parent's approval is generally good enough, so long as the child's health is not endangered.

Loitering—S. 54, The Child Welfare Act, 1978: Although the offence of vagrancy has been withdrawn from Canada's Criminal Code for persons under the age of sixteen, the offence of loitering remains. Technically, that person cannot be in a place to which the public has access between the hours of 10 o'clock in the evening and 6 o'clock in the morning unless accompanied by a parent or adult specifically appointed by the parent. Although a private party is not a place of public access, driving or walking home becomes a problem. At one time, it was thought that this Section would be repealed, but, with the emergence of the Yonge Street Strip in downtown Toronto, this Section was needed to assist the police in "cleaning up" where, for want of this provision, they would have no authority.

Payments for Adoption—S. 67, The Child Welfare Act, 1978: This Section now makes it an offence if any person, either before or after the birth of a child, makes, gives or receives, or agrees to make, give or receive any payment or reward in consideration of any work facilitating the process of the adoption, including the signing of consents, the transfer of custody, or the conducting of negotiations. The Section does not apply to the payment of expenses by an adoption agency, or to the payment of legal expenses in connection with an adoption. It remains to be seen whether this Section will curb the existence of "adoption-brokerage" businesses.

The concern of all these provisions, whether under the *Criminal Code* or the *Child Welfare Act, 1978*, is the welfare and protection of children. The difference between the two, practically speaking, is the degree of societal sanction: the Code represents punishment and deterrence and to some extent, rehabilitation, while the *Child Welfare Act* is primarily designed to provide for rehabilitative assistance only. Practically, the difference is one of degree, because child welfare proceedings often have the effect of punishment, with the removal of the child as retribution and as a deterrence to faulty parenting. However, if it is punishment or deterrence that is desired by the State, then the *Criminal Code* and not the *Child Welfare Act* should be invoked; putting a parent in jail or taking the child from his home does not help the child other than ensuring minimum protection.

One of the difficulties facing Children's Aid Society workers is that, unlike a Crown Attorney in criminal proceedings, they are supposed to be the therapist and prosecutor at the same time. Each role practically thwarts the other. In one case, for example, a father had indecently assaulted his fifteen-year-old daughter, who then went to live in a children's mental health facility. The father's lawyer advised his client that the daughter should have no contact with him or his family until the matter had been determined at trial. The daughter did not want her father sent to prison, but desired only that he be helped and that she continue seeing the rest of her family while under treatment. Incest is such a serious taboo that the *Criminal Code*, as well as the *Child Welfare Act* enters the picture. To imprison the father may satisfy the law but the child's advocate must primarily concern himself with reuniting the child to her father and family and give her the opportunity to work out her feelings about her father. The *Criminal Code* may satisfy the protection of property by way of imprisonment or fine. However, a child is not property, and although a taboo may have been broken, protection of the child through punishment must be reconciled with an appreciation of the parent-child dynamic.

In too many situations, the child is treated like any other witness, without any additional resources available to assist the family and the child prior to and following the hearing. In this case, outside professionals were engaged for fourteen months prior to the trial. At trial, the court suspended sentence but placed the father on probation, directing family counselling as a requirement and asking the counsellor to monitor visits among father, daughter and family. In other words, the child was not exiled from her family while the father was being treated.

What is a Child?

When children are the "criminals", twentieth-century values of childhood underlie not only the disposition, which seeks helping rather than punishing, but also the attribution of responsibility. A child cannot be convicted of an offence while he is under the age of seven years. If he is between the age of seven and fourteen years, the court must be persuaded that the child did commit the unlawful act and intended to do it. Also, the court must find that the child had the ability to know the nature of his act, and its consequences: the child had to appreciate that the act was a wrong one. One Family Court in Ontario has ruled that this last factor requires greater evidence of understanding than simply the child's knowledge that something is "wrong", a test applied when an adult raises insanity as a defence. According to that ruling, there is an obligation upon the prosecution, if the defendant is between the ages of seven and fourteen years, to show the child's capacity to comprehend the moral implications of his act. It must also be shown that he knew beyond a reasonable doubt the wrongful nature and the consequences of his activities. This test suggests that the court consider the motivations of the child and his cognitive ability, applying a principle of diminished responsibility which is not technically available to persons fourteen years or older.

However, once an accused is found to be able to distinguish between right and wrong, he is sane for criminal-law purposes and responsible for his actions without further examination of his motivation or understanding. In one case, an eleven-year-old admitted to the police that his job was to stand on guard, while his friend, age twelve, pocketed various items from a candy store. The court refused to accept the child's story that he was unaware of the consequences of his "guard duty". In another case, a child who just turned seven caused damage to property in the amount of approximately \$85,000. He had thrown matches down an eavestrough while he was sitting on a garage roof, unaware that there were old clothes soaked in gasoline at the foot of the piping. The child, through his counsel, raised the argument that he was playing a game of "rocketships" and had no idea that a fire would result. However, neither the victim, out-of-pocket by some \$85,000, nor the Judge, as it happened, felt moved enough to diminish this child's responsibility.

Age is considered in determining not only criminal liability, but the degree of liability as well. For example, a seven-year-old child shot and killed a playmate and was charged with having committed a delinquency by allegedly causing death by criminal negligence. The court found the accused child to be negligent in failing to take proper precautions in handling the gun, thereby committing a very serious error of judgment. However it took into account the child's age and all of the circumstances of the accident: the child was not intelligent enough to support a finding that he was *criminally* negligent. In another case, children playing on railway tracks were killed by a passing train which belonged to the defendant railway company, which was subsequently found negligent for failing to take reasonable measures to prevent the accident. The company argued, among other things, that by reason of the existing statutory prohibition against persons working on the tracks, the children had violated the law and were trespassers and therefore the company should not be held liable. However, because the company failed at trial to obtain a finding as to the children's capacity to commit a crime, the court was forced to presume that the children, aged seven and nine years, did not have sufficient capacity to know they were doing wrong. In effect, the Court ruled that young children can be exempted from the Section in the Criminal Code which provides that ignorance of the law is not a defence. Knowledge of the wrongdoing cannot be presumed when children are concerned.

Perhaps the most structured attempt to transmute our values surrounding childhood—its alleged innocence, immaturity, naivety or curiosity—into legal concepts is our use of a separate code of justice for juveniles who are alleged to have committed crimes. The code, known as the *Juvenile Delinquents Act*, is a Federal Statute which defines a juvenile delinquent as:

> Any child who violates any provision of the Criminal Code or any Federal or Provincial Statute, or any by-law or ordinance of the municipality, or who is guilty of sexual immorality or similar form of vice, or who is liable by reason of any other act, to be committed to an industrial school or juvenile reformatory under any Federal or Provincial Statute.

"Child" is defined as any boy or girl actually or apparently under the age of sixteen years, but each Province has the authority under the Act to set its own upper age limit. Thus, one finds the following variations across Canada:

> Newfoundland, British Columbia: seventeen years;

> New Brunswick, Nova Scotia, Prince Edward Island, Ontario, Yukon, Northwest Territories, Saskatchewan: sixteen years;

> Manitoba and Quebec: eighteen years;

> Alberta: sixteen years for boys and eighteen years for girls.

The court must confirm the age of a child under the *Juvenile Deliquents Act*, otherwise any finding of delinquency can be set aside and a new trial ordered. Evidence as to his *actual* age might include testimony by the mother or evidence of a father testifying as to his wife's pregnancy, his attendance with her at the hospital upon delivery of the child, and his taking home of the same child whom he was shown as a newly-born infant. A certificate of birth issued under the *Vital Statistics Act* is also acceptable. *Apparent* age can be deduced through such variables as a child's physical appearance, what the child was brought up to believe as his date of birth, or evidence of the child's mental development or stage of education based on his level of writing or conversation.

One British Columbia court has held that if a child aged fifteen-and-a-half commits an offence, for example, in Alberta where the age limit is sixteen years, but the child resides in British Columbia where the age is seventeen years, the proper court is that of British Columbia. Is it a denial of "equality before the law" when one child is "helped" as a juvenile in one province and "punished" as an adult in another? Or, is it a denial of equality before the law that Alberta defines "child" as boys under sixteen and girls under eighteen? Apparently, the "best interests of children" override guarantees in our Bill of Rights to "equality before the law".

Looking at the definition of a "juvenile delinquent" it is possible for a child to be guilty of juvenile delinquency, thereby acquiring a criminal record on the basis of nothing more than a finding of guilty for "sexual immorality of similar form of vice". Accordingly, and absurdly, children who are promiscuous, truant, or smoking under age, share the same label as those who break and enter, steal or rape. While the assumption underlying the broad definition of "juvenile delinquent" is that the sentence will fit the crime, it must be realized that in areas such as Northwestern Ontario where facilities are minimal, children can be placed in a maximum security setting for no offence greater than truancy, sharing their "rehabilitative process" with the thief and the rapist.

The Punishment and The Crime

The Judge is restricted to specific dispositions as outlined in the Act. Other than placing the child, referred to as a "committal", he or she may:

(1) Suspend final disposition;

(2) Adjourn the hearing or disposition of the case from time to time for any definite or indefinite period;

(3) Impose a fine not exceeding $25.00 which may be paid in periodic amounts or otherwise;

(4) Allow the child to remain in his home, subject to the visitation of a probation officer, the child to report to the court or to the probation officer as often as may be required; or

(5) Impose upon the child such further or other conditions as may be deemed advisable.

This last remedy should not be used to commit a child. However, it has been employed to restrict a child from driving a car if perhaps he had been driving while impaired. It has also been used to order a child to take part in a restitution program where he works within the community, paying off his debt for damaging property.

A Family Court Judge in Ontario invoked this remedy to direct a child to attend a private school for children with learning disabilities. It was argued that the child's "acting out"—the repeated thefts of cigarettes—was directly related to his frustration at constantly failing in school, and therefore the school system had not responded to his learning needs. When we think of the number of inmates in our jails who have a history of learning handicaps and are caged up largely because adequate learning facilities were not available, we can only hope that this case sets a precedent. A sentence which confronts the roots and not merely the symptoms of criminal behaviour reflects the best use of the powers of assistance available to the child under the *Juvenile Delinquents Act.* Unfortunately, sentences like this one are so far rare—almost non-existent.

The court went on to order the Municipality to pay the costs of the private schooling, some $7,800 for the year. Here, the court relied on section 20(2) of the Act, finding that since the child's parent could not afford it, public resources were needed. Here, as seemed inevitable, the case bogged down. Mention money, costs, and whammo, so much for all the nice talk about a child's rights and best interests. The case is now under appeal, the Municipality protesting all the way; but meanwhile they *are* paying, and the child *is* learning. This fourteen-year-old who, under the public school system, could not read street signs is now reading books. It's a happy ending, so far.

If application is made under S. 16 of the *Juvenile Delinquents Act*, the court may postpone or adjourn the hearing of a charge of delinquency indefinitely, or for such period as the Court may advise. This section may be relied upon *prior to the adjudication of delinquency* on the basis that a finding is not necessary; the child, so to speak, has learned his lesson. The Section is usually only successfully invoked if the child has no previous record and the court can be persuaded that a finding of juvenile delinquency is not necessary in view of the child's "voluntary" reformed conduct.

Committal of the child is a disposition available to the court only upon a finding of delinquency. If the crime is serious, or the child needs a confining setting or a residential treatment setting, the court may order him to be placed in a designated setting and detain him there for a definite, or more likely, an indefinite period of time. To accomplish this, the court may commit the child to the care and custody of a probation officer, or any other suitable person which includes the Director of a group home. The court may also direct that the child be placed in a suitable family home, or commit the child to a training school or the Children's Aid Society. In making this decision the court is bound by the wording of the Statute which dictates that the action taken shall ". . . in every case be that which the Court is of the opinion is for the child's own good and what the best interests of the community require".

Once a child is committed to a Children's Aid Society or a training school, he is no longer subject to the Federal *Juvenile Delinquents Act*, and is thereafter governed by the Provincial

Child Welfare Act, 1978, or the *Training Schools Act*. This is important because under Canada's *Juvenile Delinquents Act* the court, upon application by the child, has the right to cause a further hearing to be held at any time in order to review the child's status. Under the two Provincial Acts, there are limitations which restrict this avenue of review, an avenue which can be essential. In one case, the child persisted in running away from his placement. Upon application to the court for review, it was learned, after lengthy examination of the other inmates, that the child was the victim of gang abuse at the placement. Here, the child was able to effect the change himself, justifying his escapes to a receptive court, with the help of counsel.

Training School

The most severe disposition which a Judge can make is committal to a training school and (aside from doing so under the *Juvenile Delinquents Act*) the Judge may only do so under the Provincial *Training Schools Act* if the child is twelve or more, but under sixteen, and if the child has committed an offence which would be punishable by imprisonment if he were an adult. The infamous Section 8 of Ontario's *Training Schools Act*, which allowed a committal even if the child had committed no offence, was repealed in 1975. Where a child is committed to a training school, he becomes a ward of that school, and subject to the guardianship of that school's superintendent. During this time, the rights and duties of the child's parents or any other guardian are suspended. This process is similar to that created by a committal to a Children's Aid Society which, like the training school superintendent, becomes the guardian when the child is made its ward. The training school committal is distinctly different from committal to the care, custody and control of a probation officer, a suitable person or a foster home. In these cases, guardianship remains with the parents.

Once a child is committed to the training school system, he remains a ward until he attains the age of eighteen years, unless the Minister of Community and Social Services orders otherwise. Wardship will continue even when the child is returned home on probation, unless, again, the Minister directs otherwise. Although the *Training Schools Act* limits children who may be committed to a training school to those of at least twelve years of age and under sixteen years of age, the *Juvenile Delinquents Act* provides that a child can be committed to a training school between the ages of seven and twenty-one. The Acts work independently of one another, and it is therefore possible, under the *Juvenile Delinquents Act*, for a child to be placed in a training school up to the age of twenty-one years.

Training schools in Ontario are slowly being phased out of operation, having been found less than effective, if not detrimental to the needs of children in trouble. However, until they disappear, a brief review of the child's rights within the system is helpful.

Each training school will often have an internal review board which assesses children for possible release similar in its operation to a parole board. It makes decisions without representations from the child or the parents or by their legal representatives. However, the Board will review information by any party, including collected independent reports. At their meetings, the information will likely be presented by the attending child care worker, the consulting psychiatrist, and the after-care officer. If a home placement is contemplated, an inspection report will be submitted. The Board will meet within sixty days of the child's admission, and every ninety days thereafter.

In addition to the internal review board, the regulations to the *Training Schools Act* provide a Training School Advisory Board. The Board meets every week in Toronto to review cases presented by the superintendent of the various schools, which may or may not rely upon the machinery of an internal review board. The superintendent will refer to the Training School Advisory Board any recommendations that the child remain in the school for a further period, that the child be placed in a home away from the school, or that there be a termination of the training school wardship. Upon reviewing these recommendations, the Training School Advisory Board will make a recommendation to the Minister. It is important to realize that the Advisory Board simply makes recommendations and the Minister makes the decisions. Because it acts in an advisory capacity, it is under no duty to provide an opportunity for counsel for the child to attend, or to allow the child or counsel access to reports concerning the child.

Wards of the training school system are entitled to send and receive correspondence, but they may be read by an authorized superintendent who may stop any letter if, in his opinion, the contents are contrary to the best interests of the child or of the recipient. An exception is made in the case of letters from a solicitor, the Minister, the Deputy Minister, members of the Ontario Legislative Assembly, members of the Parliament of Canada, or the Office of the Ombudsman. In fact, these letters are to be forwarded without delay. Similarly, with visitation rights, the superintendent uses his discretion but will generally respect solicitor/client relationships.

Where a child is placed by the training school, either at home or in an alternative placement, an after-care officer will be appointed to supervise the child's activities. It appears that the after-care role continues for a one year period before the Training School Supervisory Board, on its own initiative, or with the recommendation of the superintendent, will consider the termination of wardship. Where a child is placed at home as part of the one year supervision, his wardship continues and guardianship remains vested in the superintendent of the training school to which he was committed.

The superintendent is to notify the child and his parent or guardian when wardship is to be terminated. The child's records remain with the superintendent and will not be released to a lawyer or a parent of the child unless so ordered by the court, or if a child of majority age (eighteen years in Ontario) has provided the appropriate release. These records are kept some twenty years following the termination of the wardship.

Which Court?

However serious the offence, the *Juvenile Delinquents Act* does not permit the Judge to "incarcerate" the child as if it were an adult sentence of imprisonment. However, if a child is over the age of fourteen, and commits an indictable offence under the Criminal Code, he may be liable to the transfer of this case to the adult court. The Crown Attorney must apply to the Juvenile Court and the Juvenile Court Judge may, in his discretion, order the child to be proceeded against in the adult courts, but may at any time before such proceeding has commenced, rescind any order so made. A transfer of a child from the Juvenile Court to the adult court may only occur if the crime is of a most serious nature, and the criminal and other record of the child supports no other recourse or solution. Otherwise, the matter is heard in the Family Division of Provincial Court.

Where the matter is heard in the Family Court, pursuant to the *Juvenile Delinquents Act*, S. 3(2) of the Act provides that a child adjudged to have committed delinquency is to be dealt with, not as an offender, but as one in a condition of delinquency and requiring help and guidance and proper supervision. Section 38 instructs us that the Act is to be liberally construed in order that its purpose may be carried out, which is, according to that Section "... that the care and custody and discipline of a juvenile delinquent shall approximate as nearly as may be that which should be given by his parents, and so far as is practical every juvenile delinquent shall be treated, not as a criminal, but as a misdirected and misguided child, and one needing aid and encouragement, help and assistance".

This may seem fair enough, but I have found in my experience that neither of these Sections is of much assistance in locating non-existent resources for a "helping" disposition. I used to think it was a question of lack of money. I am now more inclined to believe that acting as a "parent" for a "misdirected and misguided child", one who needs "aid, encouragement, help and assistance" in our society, means locking the child up, depriving him of various freedoms, and essentially getting rid of the "problem" from the family. The gentle wording of the Act is of little consolation to a child who is locked up indefinitely for a first offence of break and enter, or even more unjustly, for the "offence" of truancy.

For that reason, it is essential to realize that the juvenile delinquency hearing is a two-stage process, first one of adjudication, and then, disposition. *And, without an adjudication of delinquency based on evidence proving beyond reasonable doubt that a child has committed an offence, the Court has no power to make any decision with respect to disposition.*

Many courts consider that proceedings under the *Juvenile Delinquents Act* be treated less formally than those under the criminal system, and indeed, S. 17 of the Act provides that proceedings "... may be as informal as the circumstances will permit, consistent with the due regard to the proper administration of justice". When one considers the not so "informal" consequences of a delinquency finding, stringent regard for proper procedure and fair play in the court room becomes foremost when representing a child before a court. Presented below are various guidelines, the breach of which stresses "informality" to the point of abuse of process:

(1) Prior to the adjudication of delinquency, a Judge's knowledge of the child's background should come solely from the evidence presented at trial;

(2) The accused, or counsel on his behalf, should be informed of the substance of any probation report or pre-sentence report or any statement insofar as it is detrimental to the child so that he may have an opportunity in open court to agree with it, explain it, or deny it. All statements which are prejudicial to the child, and which he denies should be open to cross-examination. If the court does not consider the matter to be important enough to justify formal proceedings, the statement should be ignored altogether.

(3) All information assisting the Judge in his disposition should be introduced and considered in open court in the presence of the child or his counsel, giving them

every opportunity to challenge or contradict.

(4) A child should always be entitled to make his answer in defence, to lead evidence, and to call witnesses on his own behalf.

(5) Intervention by a Judge during the examination of witnesses should be done sparingly and only for limited purposes. The Judge should *not* "descend into the arena".

(6) A child, like any other person, is entitled to a presumption of innocence unless the evidence proves otherwise "beyond a reasonable doubt".

Unique to the Juvenile Court proceeding and reflective of its protective approach is the statutory direction that the trial should take place without publicity and that any trial of a child should be held separately and apart from the trial of other accused persons. As well, any report of the delinquency committed or said to have been committed by a child, or any charge against an adult having contributed to a child's juvenile delinquency, is not to be disclosed for the purpose of publication without leave of the court. Any information as to the child's name, institution in which he was residing, the school he attended or the name of parents should similarly not be disclosed.

Whether or not such privacy is in the best interests of the child is debatable. However, the fact that the hearings are held in private should not deter counsel from acting as aggressively in the name of the child's civil liberties as if he were representing an adult. If the child is adjudged a juvenile delinquent, the court has remedies within its power which rival and sometimes even surpass those of the adult court. The only real guarantee to the child under the *Juvenile Delinquents Act* is that he cannot be "incarcerated"; that is, put in jail for his actions. But, being "committed" or "incarcerated" can be a matter of semantics. Being drugged and locked up indefinitely in a separate facility is a deprivation of the child's civil liberties, as much as if we were to toss him in jail. Various courts have held that a sentence which is not definite in terms of the time to be served (which for an adult is perhaps two years) is not a violation of "equality before the law" as guaranteed by the Canadian Bill of Rights, since the intent of the Federal legislation is to deal differently with children. So the fact that children can be more severely punished than adults is not a violation of the Bill of Rights! Would any of today's adult minorities tolerate such a raw deal?

One case in particular comes to mind in which the child, diagnosed as "full of anger and a depressive-aggressive", had been placed in a residential setting specifically to deal with such difficulties. One day this fourteen-year-old child "acted out" against her Children's Aid social worker. The next thing she knew, she was standing before the court on a charge of assault. The social worker wanted to have the child found a delinquent and to give the court supervision of the child until she was twenty-one years old. (Once a child of whatever age is adjudged a "juvenile delinquent", the brand stays with him until he is twenty-one, whether or not he is ever involved with the law again.) The Judge presiding was not pleased with this haste and insensitivity:

> While just looking at the situation, this is a ward of your Society, temporary ward, and for what must be obvious reasons it would seem fit to place her in Thistletown. She is in therapy, and psychiatrists are qualified people with different kinds of skills who would obviously, I would assume, have an insight into "L" that none of us would have from their own point of view. I ask you again, do you think it would have been wise to consult with the psychiatrist who is her therapist, before laying such a charge?[2]

In this, a clear relationship between therapy and a finding of "guilty" or "not guilty" all but disappears. Treatment, not guilt, becomes the pivotal issue. If the child acted out against the kind of treatment she was undergoing — to be expected in a therapeutic situation — then in what way was she delinquent? Unbelievably, many representatives working for children often say that bringing a child to court when the child "acts out" is useful as an additional means of treatment. They feel that the scenario enacted in court reminds the child of responsibilities, his duty to cooperate with authority.

But the Judge is an arbitrator of law, not the ultimate social worker. The courtroom is not designed for enacting therapeutic scenarios or making up for inept therapy sessions. If the young woman is found guilty of assault as charged, she may be reminded of her responsibilities, but she will also, more seriously, come out with a criminal record. And then no amount of "best interests" can protect her from the stereotypical reaction of agencies and authorities to the neatly stamped and labelled "juvenile delinquent".

Cautions, Admissions and Confessions

The procedure for the arrest of a child and the obligation of the child to supply information concerning his name and address is the same as that of adults. If the child does not give his name or address, he may force a police officer to exercise his discretion one way or the other about "reasonable and probable grounds" for arrest. The child, by protesting, may undermine any benefit of the doubt he might have achieved by simply providing this kind of information. This is especially true for children since "cautions" are often used by the police force when children are involved. A "caution" is an informal warning which often involves contact between the police and the parents. Where the police officer is prevented from following this less serious route because of the child's refusal to disclose his name or residence, the officer may rely on the process of arrest and laying of charges.

If a child is arrested, or simply detained, two issues commonly arise; namely, the protection of the child's civil rights and the inadmissability in court of involuntary statements. In accordance with the Canadian Bill of Rights, a child should have the right, as a participant in the criminal process, to be informed immediately of the reason for his arrest. The child should also have the right to retain and instruct counsel immediately, and to pursue *habeas corpus*, a remedy available to all Canadians to question the validity of their detention and to seek release if unlawfully detained.

The right to retain counsel without delay is all the more important since there is as yet no clear rule of law that demands that a parent or a person *in loco parentis* be present when a statement is taken from a child. It has been held, however, that a child cannot waive his rights during interrogation to retain and instruct counsel, no matter how well-intentioned the police or persons in authority, unless a parent or an equivalent is, in fact, present.

The second issue, that of the inadmissability of involuntary statements, arises when children give incriminating statements without fully appreciating their legal predicament. Unlike the situation in the United States, no constitutional guarantees exist in Canada which compel an assessment of the voluntariness of statements from the perspective of protection of rights. Voluntariness of a child's statement in Canada is determined *ad hoc* by way of a special hearing within the context of the juvenile hearing.

Nevertheless, it has been traditionally suggested that, in taking statements which may be incriminating, children are not to be dealt with as adults: it is not sufficient to caution a child and ask him if he understands the caution. The police officer must demonstrate to the court that the child did in fact understand the caution and its consequences as a result of careful explanation. When a mentally retarded child, just over fourteen years of age, was charged with murder, the mere reading of the caution was found to be "an empty performance" given the capacity of the child. Nowhere, in this particular case, was it brought home to the child that he might be charged with murder and not simply as a juvenile delinquent. The giving of the caution, formidable and overwhelming to a child, did not remove the child's impression that he was obliged to answer the questions of the police. Furthermore, the courts consider that relatives ought to be present if a child is to be questioned and asked to make a statement, particularly if the child asks that his parents or relatives be present.

In one particular Quebec case, the court suggested a number of guidelines in taking statements from children to ensure the voluntary giving of information. The guidelines are not rules of law, but have been frequently referred to as recommended procedure:

(1) Require that a relative, preferably of the same sex as the child to be questioned, accompany the child to the place of interrogation;

(2) Give the child, at the place or room of the interrogation in the presence of the relative who accompanies him, the choice of deciding if he wishes his relative to stay in the same room during the questioning, or not;

(3) Carry out the questioning as soon as the child and his relative are at headquarters;

(4) Ask the child, as soon as the caution is given, whether he understands it, and if not, give him an explanation; and

(5) Take the child, if it is impossible to proceed immediately, to a place exclusively for use by children and adults.

The rules noted above should apply to any person of authority, making it unacceptable for a student to be interviewed by a police official unless at least one of his guardians is present. A principal or teacher, being in positions of authority, should not assume this parental responsibility. In one American case, the question of voluntariness arose in the context of a therapeutic session. A child admitted the commission of a criminal act in a group therapy session held at the juvenile institution. The children had been directed by the supervisor to admit freely all anti-social activities including criminal acts. The child understood that failure to cooperate in a group session could result in further curtailment of his freedom, including a transfer to a less desirable youth facility. In view of these facts, the juvenile's admissions were held inadmissable in evidence in the absence of the more stringent procedure safe-guarding statements upon arrest, known in the United States as the "Miranda Warning".

Where a matter proceeds to trial, the child must be put in a separate facility used exclusively by children. As in the case of an adult charged with a crime and initially detained, a child, charged and detained pursuant to the *Juvenile Delinquents Act*, has the right to bail. However, the accused child needs an adult to sign the undertaking. A friend under the age of eighteen will be of no help. As we will discuss in Chapter 4, various rules exist which limit the ability of a child to contract. The signing of a bail recognizance by a child on behalf of an accused person is a contract which is considered not to be for the benefit of the child, and is therefore void.

Where the matter does proceed to trial, notice of the hearing must be served on the parents or guardians of the child, or, if there is neither a parent or a guardian known, on some near relative of the defendant child. The court may give appropriate directions as to notice to other persons if the parents or guardians are unavailable. In the absence of such notice, the court has no jurisdiction to proceed and any finding of delinquency will be set aside. As well, notice to the parent or guardian must inform him not only of the date of the hearing but also of the charge.

Various American studies suggest that our rehabilitative programmes for delinquent children have no effect in dealing with their needs. If these studies are correct, we are spending daily rates of up to $93 to house "problem children" without any likelihood of alleviating their disposition towards crime. Some argue for a more humane correctional system. Others throw their arms up, tired of the sentimentalist's liberal approach, and point out that children are "conning" the juve-nile courts, that what is needed is a legal system which metes out more down-to-earth judicial punishment and less social-work sophistry. The debate never ends, and the existing *Juve-nile Delinquents Act* (around since 1904) is the subject of repeated attempts at legislative revision.

In the meantime, we are growing slowly more aware of the dynamics by which a delinquent child interacts with the world, and of the root causes of his or her behaviour. It is no secret that the first world of any child is his family, and his connection with the family must first be understood if we are to make any sense of aberrant actions. The law accepts the family's importance, and in the next chapter we will see how Canada's legal system helps and hinders the interests of our children in the home.

2

THE FAMILY IN CONFLICT

Jamie: She moves up to me, throws me into the car, and I can't move, you know, because she has my hands like this; and I start trying to kick for the gear shift, but I must have been kicking at it diagonally because it wouldn't move. And they had binoculars in the car; binoculars in the car. So can you see how this was planned out, and I couldn't get off . . . this is the roadway here, and they are on the wrong side of the street.

His Lordship: I understand now.

Jamie: Can't you see how planned out that was? Because there was only one spot like that that he could do that. All the other spots can run out onto somebody's lawn, and even if there was no thorn bushes on the other side, I wouldn't have had enough time to climb it; and there was . . . did you know about this Greek man?

His Lordship: Yes.

Jamie: He was walking by and he didn't do anything, and he says he knew that I was being kidnapped. He didn't even help me.

His Lordship: I saw him yes, he was there.

Jamie: I was kicking and screaming. Did he say what I said or was he not allowed?

His Lordship: No, you see, you have certain rules in the court and I have to go by the rules, but I think now — I have my notes, I think he said that you were, you were just shouting and screaming. I think he said that. I would have to look at my notes to be sure.

—*Excerpt of interview in Chambers between a Justice of the Ontario Supreme Court and a child, subject of a custody proceeding.*[3]

The law has good intentions when it intervenes in family life to protect children, but very often the rights of the child run head-on against the rights of the adults, who are more powerful and clever at manipulating the rules. It may come as a shock to realize that, under certain circumstances, the kidnapping of children in a custody fight is seen as a justifiable action under the law. Note that Section 250 of Canada's *Criminal Code* provides:

1 Everyone, who with intent to deprive a parent or guardian or any other person who has lawful care and charge of a child under the age of fourteen years of the possession of that child, or with intent to steal anything on or about the person of such a child, unlawfully,

(a) takes or entices away or detains a child; or

(b) receives or harbours a child;

is guilty of an indictable offence and is liable to imprisonment for ten years;

2 This Section does not apply to a person who, claiming in good faith the right to possession of a child, obtains possession of the child.

The kidnapping parent may love the children, and may indeed have a "right" to snatch them away, but what of the psychological damage done to a child spirited away by one parent during a custody fight? How can he learn to trust either parent again; what does such an action do to his development? And don't forget that a court order is needed to get the child back, for the kidnapper is apparently respected by our system as a person "claiming in good faith the right to possession of a child."

The Child as Property: Kidnapping and Other Strategies

Bill C-51, 1977-78 Can., an Act to amend the Criminal Code in the *Canada Evidence Act* and the *Parole Act* would repeal S. 250 and enact a more comprehensive Section, a portion of which is to read:

Everyone who being the parent or guardian of a child

under the age of fourteen years
  (a) takes or entices away, conceals or detains or receives
      or harbours that child in contravention of a custody
      or access provision of a custody order in relation to
      that child made by a court anywhere in Canada; or
  (b) where there is no custody order in relation to that
      child made by a court anywhere in Canada, takes or
      entices away, conceals or detains, or receives or
      harbours a child with intent to deprive a parent or
      guardian or any other person who has the care or
      charge of that child of the possession of that child,
      unless the parent, guardian or other person from
      whose care or charge the child was taken or kept had
      consented to the taking, detention, confinement
is guilty of an indictable offence, and is liable to imprisonment for five years for an offence under paragraph (a) or
to imprisonment for two years for an offence under paragraph (b).

But despite the intent of the proposed amended version, in
considering the child's rights, it is important to realize that
both the present and proposed law speaks to the issue of taking
a child *away from a parent*. In abduction charges, the basic
concern is the deprivation of property. The State wants to
protect the adults' property rights; the rights of that property,
the child's rights, are incidental.

    In our example at the head of this chapter, we see an
evident violation of Jamie's civil liberties. His right to walk
home from school or to play with his friends with a sense of
safety has been abused. His experience will leave him wary and
unsure; since he is a child, his kidnapper will not likely fall
under S. 247 of the *Criminal Code*, which states that anyone
who kidnaps another person with intent to confine, imprison,
or transport against that person's will, "is guilty of an indictable offence and is liable to imprisonment for life." The child
who is kidnapped will wonder if he is a "person" at all: a piece
of property, perhaps; a pawn in the increasingly common

interspousal battle for custody. A parent is not seen as deserving punishment for kidnapping, nor is a parent seen to merit judicial, if not general, disdain for subjecting the child to the court room fray. Spousal anger, frustration, bitterness and revenge pour out in the name of the child's "best interests" so obliterating that child's voice that it is the exception rather than the rule for a judge to hear from him before deciding on his future.

In Ontario, under the *Family Law Reform Act, S.O. 1978*, a husband and wife, or a man and woman who have cohabited and have a child, may enter into a Separation Agreement which deals with the question of custody, education and moral training of their children. Any such agreement is subject to the overriding jurisdiction of the court, which might set aside any term of the agreement where it is not found to be in the "best interests" of the child. If the parties are unwilling to enter into an agreement, they may agree to mediation under the guidance of a third party. A social worker, the Chief of a Native band, or a priest might act as a mediator and divert the conflict from the court room by providing the time and structure for discussion necessary to resolve the dispute in a climate invariably more beneficial to the parties than the court room.

In one case, typical of so many others, the mother and father had separated. The mother had a history of mental illness, and the father, coincidentally a psychiatrist, desired a divorce on the grounds of mental cruelty. Moreover, as a result of the mother's alleged bizarre conduct, the father was denying the mother any access to the child. There was no shortage of allegations evidencing a situation of hurt and mistrust. It was clear that the parties would not reconcile and would live separate whether divorced or not. The critical issue was not their status as husband and wife, but as mother and father to the child of their marriage. They could not communicate with one another about their child for more than twenty seconds without an explosion. And so entered the lawyers, who substituted for their clients' open warfare, "civilized" guerilla activity in the form of "private and confidential" correspondence, affidavits and pleadings. Fortunately, before court, indeed on the way to court, the parties were able to agree upon the appointment of a third-party professional mediator, in this instance, a family counsellor, who would be empowered to meet with the parties and the child over a period of four months at a cost of $800. In this case, it worked. Access and custody are at present being exercised in a manner agreeable to the mother and father and the child. Mediation is no guarantee to the resolution of a dispute, but it should be a prerequisite to marching off to court.

In another case, embittered and destructive parents litigated their grievances before a court for 22 full days after 49 applications prior to the hearing, all because they could not get together, or get it together, to establish a structure for the father's visits to his children. The father had considered every way of getting to the kids. He had even, imaginatively, rented a horse and buggy in order to sell himself to his kids. It worked. Tying up their shoes, racing out of the door, the kids were lifted up by Sir Lancelot amidst all their friends and neighbours, who were delighting in the success of the reputedly vanquished father. After four years of post-separation fighting, thousands of dollars in costs, volumes of prepared affidavit evidence heaping allegation upon allegation, the father had penetrated through it all, reaching out to the feelings of his children on their level, rather than on the level of the adults whose approach had yielded only strife.

But the conflict, of course, continued when the children returned home. It was said that they had been tricked, and the court, after hearing of this event and "a thousand others" ordered the parties into mediation with a family psychiatrist in order to receive treatment instead of, or as part of, justice — if not justice for the adults, then at least for the children.

The wisdom of the court in not making a final order of custody or access, other than directing mediation, is a comment upon the futility of court rooms as a place to resolve a family problem. Hiring a name, putting up money, arming ourselves with a sense of justice, due process, and a right to a day in court are unfair ways of airing grievances and ending a chapter in our lives, when we consider the effect of it all on a child. As encounter therapy, the courtroom experience is a game in which everyone comes out a loser.

In a third case, the mother and father each respected one another's ability to be a good parent and, with a little pushing from their lawyers, met and discussed issues solely related to the kids, saving the question of the division of their property and other headaches for their counsel. Both wanted to have custody of the children. Both wanted, however, to avoid fighting about it. The kids were living with the mother in the family home, attending the same school. Recognizing the needs to minimize disruption for the children, the parties agreed upon joint custody. The children would live with the mother and have liberal visiting to the father, to include four weeks during the summer, one week during Christmas and March school breaks, Friday nights, and one or two days during the weekend. As well, the children could visit with the father any time they desired. The most important feature of the joint custody arrangement, and of any joint custody arrangement, was that the mother and father would be involved in all decisions relating to the children's welfare, their education, their financial security, and the need for any medical or other kinds of treatment. That is, the power that a custody order represents when granted to a parent, the right of that parent unilaterally to make decisions concerning a child's welfare, was to be shared equally between the mother and father in spite of their marital breakdown.

If a custody battle represents a power struggle, then, perhaps by analysing what power is at stake — the right to make decisions concerning different aspects of a child's welfare — these rights can be assigned in such a way to each of the parties that conflict is avoided. One Family Court Judge in Ontario has taken the approach that when there is a custody case, the parties must rebut the presumption that they are joint guardians of the child, a presumption arising from Ontario's *Infants Act*. In other words, unless one or both of the parties can persuade the court that either should have an exclusive right of decision-making, that power should continue to be in the hands of both parents regardless of with whom the child resides each day. The concept of joint custody has recently emerged in the Canadian courts, and it will likely be as success-ful a way of resolving conflict, as is the strength of the parties' commitment to do so. To date, the courts refuse to impose joint custody upon parties where there is the possibility of conflict, seemingly recognizing the need of their commitment to make such an order workable.

Custody and The Courts

If parties fail to reach an agreement, court intervention becomes a necessary evil; the court becomes an ill-equipped rescuer. The chart below sets out various processes and sup-porting legislation which deal with custody resolution. The dotted line reflects a division between the two different stand-ards that are applied in resolving custody disputes. In the first two instances, the custody decision is determined on the basis of what is in the best interests of the child. In the latter two, it is a question of whether the child's custody should be changed, since the family's standard of care for him has become unac-ceptable to society's notion of a "coping family unit".

CHILDREN AND CUSTODY

Legal Parties	Statutory Decision Making Process	Decision Making Forum
1. Husband and Wife	*The Family Law Reform Act, 1978*	Supreme, Provincial (Family Division) Unified Family, County or District Courts
	The Infants Act	Supreme, Surrogate Courts
	The Judicature Act (equitable jurisdiction)	Supreme Court
2. Parent(s) and Third parties: The Extended Family Conflict	*The Family Law Reform Act, 1978*	Supreme, Provincial (Family Division), Unified Family, County or District Courts
	The Judicature Act (equitable jurisdiction)	Supreme Court
	The Child Welfare Act, 1978 (Part IV: Adoption)	Provincial Court (Family Division)
3. Parents and the State	*The Child Welfare Act, 1978*	Provincial Court (Family Division)
	The Judicature Act (equitable jurisdiction)	Supreme Court
4. The Child and State	*The Juvenile Delinquents Act*	Provincial Court (Family Division)
	The Training Schools Act	Provincial Court (Family Division)

Where parents cannot agree upon the custody of their child, either may apply to the court under the Ontario *Infants Act* or the *Family Law Reform Act, 1978*. In both cases, the court has authority to make an interim order which, in its discretion, seems appropriate until the final determination of the matter. Under the *Family Law Reform Act, 1978*, unlike the *Infants Act*, any person can apply for custody. Under the *Infants Act*, only the parents may apply, although the court does possess the authority to award custody to any third person who is not a parent.

An application for custody can also be brought within a divorce proceeding under Canada's *Divorce Act*. Section 10 of that Act permits a court to make interim orders for custody pending the completion of the divorce proceeding, and Section 11 allows the court to make a final order. Like the *Infants Act*, an application may be brought only by the husband or wife as parties to the divorce, although the court does have jurisdiction to award custody to an appropriate third person in its discretion regarding the child's best interests.

Applications under the *Family Law Reform Act, 1978* can be brought before a Provincial Court (Family Division), a Unified Family Court (which, in Ontario exists only in Hamilton at present), a County or District Court, or the Supreme Court. Applications under the *Infants Act* can be brought in either Supreme or Surrogate Courts, and applications under the *Divorce Act* can be brought only in the Supreme Court.

While the *Family Law Reform Act, 1978* is the only Act which, in its language, limits the court's consideration to the child's "best interests", it is the test which has been adopted under the existing *Infants Act* and *Divorce Act*. Four approaches have emerged in the court's application of this test.

The first approach is based on judicial "rules of thumb" which may assist or even dictate the resolution of a custody battle. For example, courts have considered that girls of any age are presumed to be best cared for by the mother; children of infant years, of either sex, are presumed to be better cared for by the mother, while boys over the age of eight years are presumed to be better served by their father. Where a separated husband and wife are each planning to marry again, some courts have felt that stepmothers generally work out less satisfactorily than stepfathers. Naturally, these presumptions can be rebutted by individual situations.

Another rule of thumb is that between parents and a third competing parent, the natural parents are entitled to the custody of their child unless it is evident that the welfare of the child requires the severing of these fundamental rights. This presumption is modified by the overriding test of "the best interests of the child," rendering the blood tie but one factor among many to consider in assessing the welfare of the child.

The second approach involves an attempt to allocate fault between the parents and to award custody according to certain principles within the matrimonial context. An English court of appeal has best summarized its position as follows:

> It seems to me that a mother must realize that if she leaves and breaks up her home in this way, she cannot as of right demand to take the children from the father. If the mother in this case were to be entitled to the children, it would follow that every guilty mother (who was otherwise a good mother) would always be entitled to them for no stronger case for the father could be found. He has a good home for the children. He is ready to forgive his wife and have her back. All that he wishes is for her return. It is a matter of simple justice between them that he should have the care and control. Whilst the welfare of the children is the first and paramount consideration, the claims of justice cannot be overlooked.[4]

The application of this approach in Canada has been somewhat moderated so that the conduct of a parent is considered, but only as it relates to his or her ability to care for the child.

The third and most common approach to the resolution of custody disputes is that of "quantifying" the respective abilities of the parents, measuring their child-rearing assets and liabilities and awarding custody to the parent whose abilities will yield the better investment. For example, the court considers each parent's plans in terms of the suitability of living arrangements; opportunities for education; financial security; their respective employment; the amount of time each would be able to spend with the children; and their respective intentions regarding religious upbringing. By this approach, one parent's homosexuality or one parent's adultery is not a bar in itself to a successful claim for custody. The last fact would be one among several to be considered.

The fourth approach is reflected in the recent attempts of some courts to incorporate the perspective of a child into the decision making process. Accordingly, the child's needs and interests become the pivotal issue rather than the claims of the competing parents. Focussing on the dispute in this way, the court can take a flexible, rational view of the child as the paramount consideration. Consider this approach in the dissenting decision of a Justice of the Saskatchewan Court of Appeal:

> No one bothered to bring forth much information with respect to the two individuals who, of all the persons to be affected by these proceedings, least deserved to be ignored — the children. We know their names, sex and ages, but little else. Of what intelligence are they? What are their likes? Dislikes? Do they have any special inclination (for the arts, sports or the like) that should be nurtured? Any handicaps? Do they show signs of anxiety? What are their personalities? Characteristics? What is the health of each? . . . In court, no evidence was led to establish the intellectual, moral, emotional or physical needs of the child. Far from the speculation that these children are "ordinary" (whatever that means) there is nothing on which to base a reasoned objective conclusion as to what must be done for this and that child, as individuals, and not as mere members of a general class, in order that the welfare and happiness of each may be ensured and

enhanced. Nor was any direct evidence led to show which of the parents, by reason of training, disposition, charac- ter . . . and such other pertinent factors . . . is best equipped to meet the needs of each individual child . . .[5]

This fourth approach best suits our attempt to meet the inter- ests of the child if, in fact, that is what all the parties are truly seeking.

The second decision-making process based on a concept of justice between the parents may have no real connection to the needs of the child. "Justice" *may* work to satisfy the parties as husband and wife, but has little to do with the child's perception of the family situation or his needs. For example, although the law may consider that the deserting spouse is at fault for having left the matrimonial home, the child may come to a different conclusion, feeling that it is the "deserting" spouse who has suffered wrongly at the hands of the "deserted" spouse. The child's confusion is heightened by the fact that very often the spouse who is found to be at fault is depicted by the other party as "bad mommy" or "mean daddy". When the courts rely on a process of "matrimonial justice" there is too great a risk that the court, the litigants and counsel will blur the essential distinction between the roles and duties of a husband and wife, and a parent and child.

If the child is placed uppermost in these cases, more lawyers and clients might see that the adversarial process does not really lend itself to assessment of children's needs. Meeting these needs does not mean complying with a child's wishes, by the way. In some cases, courts have denied the child the oppor- tunity to be heard, feeling that the child will feel responsible for the outcome of a hearing. In court, the child often loses either way. If the verdict goes according to his wishes, he is therefore "guilty" of choosing one parent over another. If the judge rules against his wishes, the child is thus betrayed and ignored. If judges would bend a little, if lawyers would spend more time counseling the child, these fears could be avoided or minimized.

Under each of the Acts mentioned above, the court is given jurisdiction to grant access to the non-custody parent; that is, visitation rights. Except in the most extreme situations, the court will encourage access, realizing that whoever has the children and whatever happens in the marriage, children remain part of a two-parent family and have a right to be influenced in their up-bringing by both parents. A father will not be prevented from seeing his child in order that the child may develop a closer relationship with his stepfather. In fact, in one case, a mother, who had been involved in the killing of her other children, was still allowed supervised access to her remaining children. Precautionary powers were given to the supervisor, including the right to search the premises and person of the mother prior to each visit.

The fact that a child is born outside a marriage no longer precludes or prejudices the non-custodial parent from seeking access. In Ontario, the legal concept of "illegitimacy" has recently been abolished by Statute.

Custody and Guilt

As always the judicial principle of insuring visiting to both parents is not simple in practice. A child may want to spend more time with his new stepfather at the cost of the natural father's visitation time, and the courts have held that a parent is not obliged to "physically force a child out of the door and into the arms of a waiting mother or father." Where trouble is brewing in the parents' post-separation relations, the issue of visiting always emerges as the time bomb which will explode sooner or later. Father accuses mother of interfering with visits to the child; the lawyer is summoned; the law is manipulated to remind the mother that she should not have custody of the child if she cannot respect the father's visiting rights, and so on and on. For the child, the bargaining between Mom and Dad about Sunday visits has really nothing to do with the actual scheduling of his hockey practice or birthday parties. He can sense the emotional cross-currents at work, and often the cause of children's problems in a post-breakup situation is not the child mourning for the loss of a parent, but his awareness that the parents are mourning their lost marriage, the loss of their child.

When a mother and father stay in court over a long period of time, each professing love for their children under oath — as if the oath made all the difference — they'll find little scope for letting loose the anger and frustration. The court room does not encourage emotional catharsis, and the parents can only become entrenched in their bitterness, bottling it up, each hiding behind accusations and feeling that all has not been said. In these situations, despite the supposed omnipotence of the courts, parental instincts often prevail. Not surprisingly, the parties revert to kidnapping, ignoring the piece of paper that is the court order.

The courts have recently taken a further ill-fated step in the attempt to regulate parent and child relationships by the linking of access to maintenance. In one example, the father was permitted to cease maintenance payments until the mother assured suitable access to the father. Now, each time a spousal tiff disrupts access, the non-custodial parent will stem the maintenance flow, aggravating the situation even more, and the child, once again, is lost in the shuffle. Emotions and dollars are an explosive combination.

To avoid this grim situation, it is the best medicine to arrive at a clear, detailed, written agreement upon separation, thereby establishing stability through clarified expectation. Where communications between parents have broken down, a provision allowing simply for "reasonable access" won't work, and the parties will find themselves in the court room having a structure imposed upon them.

Kidnapping, as the culminating act in negotiation or litigation, frustration and failures, is most often approached as a civil rather than criminal matter. Consider the case in which father has custody of the child pursuant to an Ontario court order. The mother removes the child to Alberta without notice, and when father tries to enforce the Ontario order in the

Alberta courts, mother's defence is the child's "best interests". Generally speaking, unless the mother can demonstrate with convincing proof that her actions were justified, the Alberta court will look with great disfavour on flouting the original Order of the Ontario court. Courts want to insure that "...swift and easy modes of travel should not make it a simple matter for a disgruntled or emotional parent to take the law into his own hands and Province-hop across the country, deliberately ignoring legitimate court orders."[6]

Where a non-custodial parent has allegedly "kidnapped" a child and there is no court order with respect to custody, the aggrieved parent will likely commence proceedings for custody in the jurisdiction in which the kidnapping parent and child are found. Of course, and this is the difficulty, one must locate the parent and child, secure a lawyer in that jurisdiction, and commence an application before parent and child move on. Good luck! Once the matter is before the court, "best interest" tests will be applied, recognizing that the aggrieved parent has "de facto" custody either by an agreement, understanding, or simply by passive acquiescence of the kidnapping parent who allowed the child to remain with the aggrieved parent since the date of separation of the parties.

Thus, whether or not the parent has secured a custody order officially, the non-custodial parent can create havoc through continuing legal battles. No custody/access order is final, since changing circumstances over the times can detrimentally affect the child's environment. The non-custodial parent always has the option of varying the original order. If the process of the courts must be relied upon, use it. Self-help remedies like kidnapping put a parent in disfavour with the court. A parent, then, should insist on a clearly worded separation agreement, one which sets out a structure for visiting, one which leaves the child to work out the details with the visiting parent without negative influence from home. If this fails, then the court should be called in to clarify arrangements, defusing conflict and recrimination among parents, and minimizing guilt in the child.

The question of passports for children is often raised in kidnapping situations. In Canada, passports can be issued for a child either in the name of the parent or the child, although in the latter case, its use is limited to the child's legal guardian. That is, no child under the age of sixteen can obtain a passport in his own name for his independent use. One passport only will be issued for a child. A parent seeking to leave the country with a child whose passport is in the name of the other parent, or limited to use by the other parent, will be unable to do so. Where the custodial parent is concerned that an application for a passport may be made, he can contact the Passport Office at the Ministry of External Affairs, and on presentation of a court order or legal agreement, the child's name will be placed on a passport security list. As a result, prior to the issuance of a passport, the custodial parent will be provided with notice. In travelling to the United States, the custodial parent may ask that the child's and the non-custodial parent's name be placed on a centralized list, so that a visa will not be issued to them. In this way, should the non-custodial parent desire to live with the child in the United States, they will have to do so unlawfully, minimizing their ability to reside in that country.

The Welfare Solution

A family's deterioration can come about in ways other than separation. While remaining in a single unit, relations can disintegrate due to any combination of psychological, economical and sociological circumstances, and thereby adversely affect the quality of child care. When the situation becomes visibly critical, the lumbering apparatus of the State must intervene by way of the child welfare hearing. In this way, the child is thrust once more into the limelight, watching the various and sundry adults determine his "best interests".

Under Ontario's *Child Welfare Act, 1978* the State is empowered, through its agent, the Children's Aid Society, to intervene if it suspects a child's minimal standard of care has been breached. In emergency situations, the Children's Aid

Society, with the aid of a police officer, may, without warning, take the child to a place of safety, detaining him until the matter can be brought to court or a Children's Aid representative may enter the premises without a warrant, and if need be, by force, in order to search for and remove a child in danger. Once he is removed, the child must be brought before the court within five days in order to determine whether he is "in need of protection".

In one case, neighbours had called the police because of noise and general uncleanliness and disrepair of a home in their vicinity. The police, when they arrived, needed no warrant to enter the house, or remain there, given the sight of an eight-month-old baby with an electrical plug in her mouth, wearing a soiled diaper and playing with dog faeces. The mother sat stoned on drugs and alcohol. The seven-year-old boy and eight-year-old girl, unglued themselves from a blaring TV program and tried to pull their mother up so she would be presentable to the police. And where was Daddy? Nobody seemed to know.

The police called upon the emergency department of the Children's Aid Society and, within hours, the children had been removed and placed in an emergency foster home, mother admitted to the Emergency Ward of a hospital. In spite of father's subsequent protests, the children remained in care, until the matter of their welfare was brought before the court within five days, and in this case, on the fourth day. At that point, the Children's Aid Society was obligated to show to the court that until a full hearing was held, the children should nevertheless remain in their care. If for any reason the matter cannot proceed on a given date, the Children's Aid Society must "show cause" why any child should not be returned to his home, even before it has been determined by the court through a hearing that any child should be removed from the home for want of adequate care.

The hearing stage is invariably adjourned to a special date in view of the need for the parents and the Children's Aid Society to prepare their case, and to collect various witnesses who are often necessary in support of each party's position. At the hearing, the onus is upon the Children's Aid Society, as a party to the proceeding, to satisfy two conditions. First, it must prove that the child is "in need of protection", as defined by the *Child Welfare Act, 1978* to include:

(a) Any child who is brought, with the consent of the person in whose charge he is, before the court;

(b) Any child who is deserted, abandoned, improperly cared for, living in an unfit or improper place, associating with unfit or improper persons;

(c) Any child who is found begging, or is uncontrollable;

(d) Any child whose life, health or morals may be endangered by the conduct of the person in whose charge he is;

(e) Any child who is being denied proper medical, surgical, or remedial care or treatment because of the attitude of the person with whom he is living; or

(f) Any child whose emotional or mental development is in danger because of emotional rejection and/or deprivation of affection.

The court will apply a general "best interests" test, looking at all of the above factors to determine whether the minimal standard has been violated.

The second stage, once a condition of "in need of protection" has been found, is that of disposition. At this point, the Children's Aid Society presents evidence in order that the court may determine the degree of necessary intervention or protective care, and accordingly, choose amongst three kinds of orders. It can place the child in the care of the parent or other person, subject to the supervision of a Children's Aid Society; it can order that the child be made a Ward of the State and committed to the care and custody of the Children's Aid Society; or it can order that the child be made a ward of the Crown and be committed to the care of the Children's Aid Society. To be made a Crown ward, the most severe measure of all, means the child can be placed for adoption by the State without notice to the parents.

Unfortunately, the two distinct stages of a finding of "protection" and rendering disposition can overlap during the judicial process. By the child's very presence in the court room there is an unspoken implication that something is lacking in the child's care, and a supervisory order becomes a relatively simple method to alleviate suspicions. Recent amendments to the *Child Welfare Act* will make it incumbent on the judge to find "protection" as a necessary first stage, itemizing his reasons with no regard to possible avenues of dispositions.

The obvious and most publicized reason for children found "in need of protection" is that of physical abuse. The taboo of incest finds its way into the Child Welfare Court and is also a ground for a finding of "protection". But after physical or sexual abuse, the test becomes more difficult to satisfy. Children of persons who are living in an unfit place are alleged to be "in need of protection". Yet, the courts are reluctant to separate children from parents whose only fault may be their poverty, or their inability to find adequate housing. Prolonged drug or alcohol abuse is different, because the court can point to an obvious failing which the parents could change if they "really wanted their child". Psychological neglect or abuse usually demands professional evidence in order to substantiate the Society's position that the children are "in need of protection". It is the most difficult to prove: once we let the State intervene in the psychology of the family, most of us — not just children of poor, single parents, or alcoholics — would be under scrutiny.

It is difficult to isolate the factors of economics and our political structure from the process of finding children "in need of protection". The Child Welfare Court is traditionally a poor person's court. The rich will be able to avoid State intervention by being able to afford and have access to private resources. The mother who must work twelve hours a day in order for her family to survive economically cannot be expected to "interact responsively" with her children at the end of the day. Yet that will be expected of her should the State become involved.

The courts seem to sanction an approach which ignores

the larger social forces outside the family unit, forces which nonetheless lead to the demise of that family as a unit. Instead, the courts prefer to turn upon the individual parent, alleging fault on his or her part. For example, consider the following excerpt from a Judge of the Provincial Court in Ontario:

> . . . [counsel] made frequent references to conditions outside the home. Family benefits, upon which mother depends, provide nothing more than a subsistence allowance. Living in the Jane-Finch area of North York in an Ontario Housing unit can be an extremely frustrating, discouraging, difficult and challenging experience. There are comparatively few recreational services available in the immediate neighbourhood of mother's apartment. I have often thought of this area as being a wasteland; an almost instantaneous community with no prior history, no sustaining values, no sense of neighbourhood identification, few public supportive services, less than needed amounts of recreational services; it has been an area whose residents have had little to be proud of and few reasons to bind themselves together. Raising children in such an environment has to be more difficult than in an area that is not as deprived.
>
> These debilitating environmental factors make [the mother's] job all the more difficult. All who worked with her were aware of the community's problems and deficiencies, but understanding these factors does not relieve any parent in the neighbourhood of the necessity of meeting the emotional and discipline needs of their children. It is all very well to feel "sorry for poor Mrs. C. who has had to live in that awful area", but this does nothing to assist her.
>
> . . .

In concluding this point, I place little emphasis on the forces that play outside the home, notwithstanding the obvious emphasis that counsel attempts to place on these factors. The crux of the case in determining whether these were children in need of protection lies inside the home, not outside of it.[7]

The purpose of the *Child Welfare Act* is not to provide new families for children but to lend professional assistance in strengthening the family unit. If custody of the child is in dispute, the main criteria for removal should not reflect the State's resources as equal to or better than the parents', but stem from the distinctively different approach of removal as necessary in order to protect the child. Ontario's *Child Welfare Act, 1978* fortifies this position by requiring the judge, in determining the "best interests of the child", to assess the merits of any plan proposed by the Society that would be caring for the child, compared with the merits of the child returning to or remaining with his or her parent, and to consider the effect upon the child of any disruption of the child's "sense of continuity". We see this commitment reflected in the situation of children of retarded parents:

> First of all, the fact of low parental intelligence should not be taken as determinative in itself of the child's need for protection. Rather, the question should be one of deciding whether, in light of their individual capabilities, these parents are able to meet their parental responsibilities. If the answer to this question is no, then the judge should decide whether, given the proper assistance and intervention, the parents can be provided with the tools necessary to care adequately for their child. This issue should not be resolved by simply noting the difficulties involved in securing the needed help when the child remains within the home. The actions of persons involved in this case show that, with a coordinated effort, extensive assistance can be given to parents... Only if it is felt that the risk to the child is too great, even with outside help, should the court remove the child from the home.[8]

Considering the above two excerpts from Judges of the Provincial Family Court in Ontario, different interpretations of the Statute may lead to different emphasis on family as opposed to environmental factors. What is clear is that there is a gap in the legislation in its attempt to assist families, as a result of limited resources or lack of commitment to support the family through support to the family's environment.

This gap is epitomized in the situation of the Native child. There is a highly disproportionate number of Native children in Northern and Northwestern Ontario who are found in need of protection. One way of dealing with the matter is to work with the Native family within their environment, however different the Native family appears, however distinct its values may be to the social worker. It is necessary to recognize the cultural identity of the Native people for there to be worthwhile assistance from our culture. It also means more funds or different standards to insure that if a Children's Aid Society assists family, the staff should be capable of coping with unusual cultural needs.

A child "in need of protection" is an entire family in need of protection, although our legislation zeroes in on the child to avoid the larger issues. A Native child has his entire cultural family to consider, although we are quick to place him in a White foster-home: it's cheaper, for one thing. Most of us assume it is better for the child, but is it? In one case, a seven-year-old Native girl had been removed from her family and placed in a foster home. She was the only Native child there, and it was arranged, through the Children's Aid Society, that her long, raven-black hair be cut so she would "fit into the home better". Her Native father had to hold back angry tears when he saw the result on his first visit.

How can we provide more sensitive and available liaison people to help the child through the difficult period of adjustment? One solution available to the Children's Aid is the homemaker who remains with the child, if he is without proper supervision and is unable to look after himself. While the homemaker is with the child, the Children's Aid Society should notify or make reasonable effort to notify the parents or any person who was caring for the child immediately prior to the neglect. A homemaker's service can be made available to the child for thirty days, after which time the matter must proceed to court to determine whether the child is in need of protection and subsequent disposition.

Another tool is the non-ward agreement to which the parents and the Society are parties. The non-ward agreement directs the child to remain with the Society but either party may terminate by giving at least twenty-one days notice in writing to the other party, thereby diverting the matter from the courts and allowing the parties to work together rather than as adversaries.

If the parents give notice, and the Society objects, the latter may at that time involve the courts for a finding of neglect and formal disposition. Similar agreements can also be made concerning children with special needs, physical disabilities, mental problems, and the like. These agreements may be valid for such periods of time as the parties feel are necessary in the circumstances. These agreements are designed to provide custodial, emotional and financial support to children with special needs and should be distinguished from those in which parents are arranging temporary custodial care only. In the latter type of agreement, the non-ward agreement, a child cannot remain in the care of a Children's Aid Society for more than twenty-four months. By either arrangement, no agreement can be entered into by the parents and the Society without the consent of the child, where the child is of the age of twelve years, or where the child's consent is not required for want of capacity to consent because of a development or handicap.

Continued access to a Society or Crown ward is another method of working towards rehabilitation of the family unit. If the child has been removed, access should therefore be an integral part of any wardship order, or non-ward agreement, unless it is absolutely not in the best interests of the child, or unless adoption plans are being undertaken. Both the child (if twelve years of age or more) and the parents have the right to apply for such access during the period of wardship unless this right has been terminated judicially.

Where a disposition order is made, a parent may apply to the same court for review of the situation after the expiration of six months from the date of the order. The court will at that time apply a "best interests" test to determine whether continued intervention is necessary by the State; if not, it can terminate the order and return the child to the parents or substitute a supervising order for a previous wardship order. It should be noted that a child cannot be in the care of a Children's Aid Society for more than 24 months by way of Society wardship. Therefore, after 24 months, the child must be returned to his home or made a Crown ward.

In addition to a parent's application, the Society itself may apply to terminate wardship if the family has improved its child care capabilities. Recent amendments to Ontario's *Child Welfare Act* allow a child of twelve years of age or more to seek a review of his status after six months of care by the Society. Another amendment has given foster parents of six months or more the right to notice and the right to be heard in the case of any hearing concerning the child for whom they have been providing a home, an amendment which recognizes the contribution foster parents can make to an up-dated assessment of the child and his wishes.

Once an order of Crown wardship is made, the child may be placed for adoption without notice to the parents, requiring only the consent of the Director of Child Welfare; once the child is placed for adoption, the parents' rights to appeal or application for the termination of Crown wardship are completely extinguished. Due to this total severance of parental rights, adoption placements cannot be finalized until

(a) Any appeal from the order of Crown wardship has been determined;

(b) The period of time for commencing an appeal, namely 30 days, has expired; and

(c) The court has terminated any outstanding order of access to the child, finding alternative plans including a proposed adoption to be more beneficial to the child than the continuation of access.

Often, a child remains a Crown ward without being placed for adoption and yet parental rights have been extinguished as outlined above. In these cases, there is a duty on the Director of Child Welfare to review the situation yearly after the child has been a Crown ward for twenty-four months.

The Child and Adoption

At the hearing to determine whether a child is in need of protection, and to determine the appropriate disposition, if the child is so found, the court may hear any person with relevant evidence, including the child, the parents, a grandparent, a foster parent, a local director of the Society, or any person on behalf of the child. The court may take into consideration both present and past conduct of the parents, including their treatment of any children, their own or otherwise. After the court has heard the evidence, it will make a finding as to whether the child is in need of protection. If it does make such a finding, and prior to disposition desires further information about the parents and the child, it may order the child and any parent of the child or other person, except the foster parent, to attend for an assessment before a person specified in the order, and who, in the opinion of the court, is qualified to perform a psychological or psychiatric assessment. If a person fails to show up for the assessment, the judge is entitled to draw an adversary inference which could result in the placement of the child with someone else in the future.

As an example of a child's complex responses to adoption, let me tell you about Stephen. At five, he had been adopted by a rather well-to-do family which did the best it could, but which failed him in many ways. An agency took over when he was twelve, and from the beginning the staff sensed that Stephen was feeling cut off from his origins. The counsellor worked with his family, his adopting mother and father, and the Children's Aid Society in an attempt to put together this young man's roots. The difficulty of learning anything from Children's Aid about a child's origins, the cloud of secrecy which surrounds the basic facts, created constant obstacles, but everyone tried.

At fifteen, Stephen could no longer be handled within the treatment centre and he was moved. He spent two separate times in jail for periods of varying length. After the second incident, the staff realized more than ever that if Stephen was to break out of his patterns he would need to be in touch with his past. After much guile and probing, they were able to get a name. His mother was approached: she was reluctant to speak at first, and quite scared. She could not believe that we had found her and did not know what to make of it. She had started a new life with a new family, but after the initial shock, she became curious and even enthralled about meeting her own child.

Letters and messages were exchanged. It was arranged that Stephen should go to Toronto to meet his mother. He was now eighteen years old. His mother came with a shopping bag full of pictures, memories of the time she and her son had spent together long ago. There were pictures of Stephen as a baby, pictures of his later growth, pictures of familiar rooms and toys. Later, they visited the home in which he was born and raised, and other places where the mother had moved after financial difficulties. Then they went to the home of his foster parents.

This visit connected Stephen to his past, filling gaps in his memory, ending some of the fantasies he had dreamed up about his parents. He realized that he had come from a good home. His roots were not ugly; he was not predestined to a vicious criminal existence because of his past. As time went by, Stephen and his mother determined a realistic relationship with one another. He ultimately did not want to live with her or become a part of her family, but he continues to visit and to maintain contact with her. With this relationship strengthened in a healthy way, Stephen has been able to become closer to other people as well, and, for whatever it is worth, since meeting his mother he has had no run-ins with the law. He has returned to school, holds down a full-time job, and, considering his experiences, is doing well.

Sometimes a little research into the past can change the child's entire self-image, as happened with Christie, a Native girl adopted into a White family. The family was doing the best they could in raising her. They had run into some difficulties around normal kinds of teenage things, with a little bit extra added to it. At the agency, we found it very important to talk to Christie about her past. Apparently, she had been told a fair amount by her adopting family. She had been told about her mother, her name, and the fact that her mother had been murdered two years after she had given Christie up for adoption. Christie presented this story to us as an ugly incident in her background. It was clear that we had to work with Christie in terms of these feelings. First, we decided to check the story out, following it back to see whether it was true or not. The story in the newspapers was really quite different from the story that Christie had been told, or perhaps that Christie had created. It was not nearly as messy as we had been led to believe. We began to doubt whether this woman who had been presented to Christie as her natural mother really was. After we checked with the Children's Aid Society and hospital records, we found that, in fact, this woman was not Christie's mother, but was only related to her. As we began to unravel the mystery further, we found that Christie's mother was not murdered, nor even dead, but alive. Imagine the effect this had on Christie's perception of herself... to be able to look in the mirror without seeing everything attached to the knowledge that her mother was a drunkard and was murdered. Christie's mother was none of these things, only a young woman who, for various reasons, had had to give up her child.

Finding someone's roots is not a cure-all, though, and one must be very careful in confronting a child with his origins. I can remember one client in particular who, at the age of sixteen, had no knowledge of his family. After months of looking, we finally found his mother. There were letters and phone calls exchanged, and a week or two weeks in advance we set out a time in which he would fly out to where his mother was living and meet her. Before the planned visit, the boy went through almost intolerable strain, testing his feelings. He could not sleep. He did not eat. He generally withdrew from everything and everyone, and in particular, his adopting mother and father. The night before the planned trip, he ran away from the treatment home and did not return until a half hour before the plane was to leave.[9]

Traditionally, our adoption rules have concentrated on the natural parent(s) and the adopting parents, but as the above histories show, the silent third party — the child — is really the most important and sensitive quantity. Adoption is an act of finality, it is the substitution of the umbilical cord by a court order. S. 86 of Ontario's *Child Welfare Act, 1978* makes this abundantly clear:

(1) For all purposes, as of the date of the making of an adoption order
   (a) the adopted child becomes a child of the adopting parent and the adopting parent becomes the parent of the adopting child; and
   (b) the adopted child ceases to be the child of the person who was his or her parent before the adoption order was made and that person ceases to be the parent of the adopted child, except where the person is the spouse of the adopting parent

   as if the adopted child had been born to the adopting parent and all the rights and responsibilities of a legal guardian of the child that have vested in any adoption agency pursuant to sub-section 3 of Section 69 are terminated;

(2) The relationship to one another of all persons whether the adopted child, the adopting parents, the kindred of the adopting parents, the parent before the adoption order was made, the kindred of that former parent and any other persons shall, for all purposes,

be determined in accordance with sub-section 1.

This Section further provides that in any will or other document, a reference to a child includes the adopted child, unless the person made his will prior to proclamation of this Section on March 31st, 1977 and indicated clearly in the will an expression to the contrary. The attempts to integrate totally the adopted child into the "family tree" of the adopting family is exempted from the laws relating to incest, and the various prohibitions surrounding kinship and marriage.

Adoption is also the cheapest form of child placement of children who are subject to inadequate parenting. Instead of spending money, in many cases, to help the original family thrive, we break it up and remove the children, placing them in comfortable, middle-class families as substitutes. Indeed, and somewhat ironically, Section 88 of the *Child Welfare Act, 1978* permits the Minister to grant a subsidy to the adopting parents of a child if it is in the best interests of the child. However, in spite of our best efforts to achieve a cheap and irrevocable placement for a child, the legal label of adoption falls short of satisfying the increasingly apparent emotional needs of children to relate to a past.

So many times, adopted kids end up back in Juvenile Court as the "runners" in the system of helping kids. Runners are kids who won't accept any affection, help or treatment and so they run. Where? They don't know. From whom? They really don't know, although they blame it on the various families and institutions to which they are exposed. These runners are the Stephens and the Christies, looking for some sense of identity and continuity.

The process of adoption is not value-free. Its effect is not always as charitable as its intention. When Helen Allen advertises children for adoption in the Toronto *Star*, an invaluable service is performed, but our cultural prejudices shine through when we are shown two Native children under the headline *Twins Hunting for Happy Home*. What a sad comment on our clichéd understanding of today's Indian! And however well-intentioned we may be, adoption of Native children into white homes is a direct attack on the survival of Native culture itself. If this sounds extreme, consider that in 1975-76, approximately 45% of the children advertised in the *Star* column were Natives. With that figure, is it such an overstatement to suggest that through adoption we are subtly exterminating the fabric of Native society?

Adoption Rights Under The Child Welfare Act

Whatever prejudices colour our approach to adoption, we have the rules laid down in the *Child Welfare Act*, and it is worth reviewing the basics from the perspective of the child and his rights as a citizen. For example:

(1) An order for adoption of a child who is seven or more years of age can only be made with the written consent of that child although the court may dispense with this consent if found to be inappropriate.

(2) The court has the power to appoint a person to act as guardian of the child before or upon the hearing of the application if, in the opinion of the court, such an appointment is required to protect the legal interests of the child;

(3) Upon the hearing of an application for adoption of a child of seven or more years of age, the court must inquire into the capacity of the child to appreciate the nature of the application and shall "where applicable" hear the child;

(4) Where the court makes an adoption order, it may order that the adopted child retain the surname by which he was known immediately prior to his adoption, or assume the surname of either or both of the adopting parents and assume the given name or names as the adopting parents desire. In the case of a child fourteen or more years of age, the court will not give such an order with respect to the given or surname of the child without the written consent of the child;

(5) All of the documents which are used in an application for adoption must be sealed and filed in the office of the court and cannot be opened for inspection except upon order of the court, or by direction of the Director of Child Welfare. The Act also sets up a "Voluntary Disclosure Registry" in which an adopted child of eighteen years or more of age and the biological parent may apply to the Children's Aid Society to be registered as a person consenting to disclosure of information regarding their biological origins. When the Director receives an application by the child or the biological parent for the purpose of receiving information disclosing the child's origins, he will examine the Registry and if the names of the biological parents and the child are registered, and if he obtains consent to the disclosure of such information from the adopting parents in addition to the adopted child and the biological parents, he is under a duty to provide the Children's Aid Society with the information contained in the adoption order and the information in the Voluntary Disclosure Registry. Once the Children's Aid Society receives information from the Director, it must then provide the information to the adopted child and the biological parent, providing them also with guidance and counselling.

The Act specifically states:

Every Society shall provide guidance and counselling to persons who may be registered in the Voluntary Disclosure Registry referred to in sub-section 2.

Creation of a Voluntary Disclosure Registry is a completely new procedure in Ontario. Considering the close vote in the legislature and opposition Cabinet to those disclosure provisions, it will be necessary to monitor the policy directives thereon.

Having suggested a reversal in the priorities of the parties traditionally involved in adoption, we now consider the second party in the triangle, the "natural" parent. For the purpose of adoption, "parent" includes:

    (a) A guardian;

    (b) A person who has demonstrated a settled intention to treat a child as a child of the family; and

    (c) A person who is not recognized in law to be a parent of the child but,

        (i) has acknowledged a parental relationship to the child and voluntarily provided for the child's care and support;

        (ii) by an order of a court of competent jurisdiction or a written agreement, is under a legal duty to provide for the child or has been granted custody of or access to the child; or

        (iii) made a written acknowledgment of the facts of his or her parentage to an adoption agency.

However, "parent" does not include the Crown, a Society or a foster parent of the child.

This definition should be read with another Section of the *Child Welfare Act* which provides that the reference to a "parent" includes the mother and father of the child. The effect of the amendments is that "parent" includes initially just about everyone. In a recent Family Court decision, the court suggested that the definition includes even the father of the child conceived through an act of rape.

The interests or rights of the biological parents are initially safeguarded by the requirement of the "consent" to the adoption. An order for an adoption of a child under 18 years of age and who has not been married can only be made with the written consent, given after the child is 7 days old, of every person who is a parent, or who has lawful custody or control of the child. Any person who has given his or her consent may cancel it by a document in writing to that effect within twenty-one days after the consent is given. In the private adoption of a newborn baby, the child will be discharged on the fifth day from the hospital nursery. Therefore he is often placed in the prospective adopting home before consent can be obtained because of the seven day minimum limitation period for obtaining a parent's consent. The twenty-one day "incubator period" for parents to change their mind does not start until consent is obtained and if, within the twenty-one days, that consent is cancelled, the child, even if placed, should be returned to the parent.

Where a child has already been removed from the biological parent, and that child has become a Crown ward, only the Director of Child Welfare need provide written consent. In this instance alone, consent from a parent need not be considered. In all other cases, the courts, before making an adoption order, must be satisfied that not only will the order be in the best interests of the child, but also that every parent who has given a consent under the Act understands the nature and effect of the adoption order.

Once consent is given, and twenty-one days from the date of the consent have passed, the responsibility for the care of the child passes from the parent to the adoption authorities. A parent does have the right to withdraw a consent even after the twenty-one day period if a court is satisfied that it is in the best interests of the child that the consent be withdrawn. However, note the concern of one court with respect to such a request:

> The legislative intent is that after twenty-one days a consent to an adoption cannot be withdrawn at the will and pleasure of a natural parent making the consent. The Statute now prevents capricious and arbitrary evasion of a consent. The Section demands exploration whether the best interests of the child require the court to give leave to withdraw the consent. A child is no longer a prize to be awarded for the vacillations or changes of mind of a natural parent. The inquiry by the court is not to be hampered by the regrets or changing feelings of the natural parent.[10]

Note that where a parent is unwilling to provide the necessary consent or consent cannot be obtained, because the whereabouts or identity of the parent is unknown (for example, the rapist) the court possesses the power to dispense with the requirement to obtain consent if satisfied that it will serve the best interests of the child. However, the court cannot do so unless proper notice for the adoption application has been served on the person withholding his consent, or, at least, that a reasonable effort has been made to notify him or her if the whereabouts are unknown.

Because the effect of an adoption is irrevocable, dispensing with the consent of a parent cannot be made except for the most compelling reasons. The judge must conclude that the person has abandoned his child or has misconducted himself in such a manner as to make his consent unnecessary. "Abandoned" has been defined as, "leaving children to their own fate, not knowing where they are or under what conditions they are living". In one case, a parent who had attempted successfully to see his children, had sent them Christmas gifts, and supported his wife and children until his wife remarried, and had retained counsel to oppose the proceedings to dispense with his consent, was found to have a very real interest in the children. Because he might at some future time establish a relationship with them, the application to dispense with his consent was denied, thereby suspending the application for adoption.

Once an adoption order is made, the only remedy available to a parent is that of appeal on these grounds:
communicate with, remove or attempt to remove from his home, or interfere with the child in any way, or do any action to the same unless it is under the direction of the Director of Child Welfare.

Once an adoption order is made, the only remedy available to a parent is that of appeal on these grounds:
   (a) The adoption is not in the best interests of the child; or
   (b) The court has not dispensed with the parents' consent, or refused the application to withdraw same.

The third side of the adoption triangle is the placement agency. As a result of the amendments to the *Child Welfare Act*, this is referred to as either the "adoption agency", a charitable corporation incorporated for the purpose of placing children under eighteen years of age for adoption, and including a Children's Aid Society, or a "licensee", an individual provided with a license for the purpose of placement of a child for adoption. No person other than an adoption agency or a licensee is entitled to place, or cause to be placed, a child under eighteen years of age with another person for the purpose of adoption. In all cases of adoption, a home study of the proposed adopting parent(s) is a necessary prerequisite subject to exceptions. The exceptions occur where the application for adoption is by a relative of a child, or by a spouse of the child's parent. A relative includes a grandparent, uncle or aunt, whether the relationship is of whole blood, half blood or by marriage, and notwithstanding that the relationship is traced through or to a person born outside marriage, or that the relationship depends on the adoption of any person. When the adoption is by a relative of the child, or by the spouse of the child's parent, the adoption may also be arranged without the assistance of an adoption agency or licensee. However, all adoptions in Ontario are effected through court order, thus subjecting the process to some degree of judicial scrutiny. In fact, the court retains the power to direct the Child Welfare Department to conduct a home study. If, as a result of the home study, the court has some reservations, it may postpone the determination of the application, making any necessary custody order for a period not exceeding one year as a "probationary period" in order to allow further assessment.

Except in the case of a joint application by a husband and wife, a court cannot make an order for the adoption of a child by more than one person, and, in fact, an order cannot be made unless both spouses give written consent. The court does have the power to dispense with such consent if the spouses are living apart and the adoption is in the best interests of the child. As well, unless special circumstances exist, the court will not make an adoption order if the application is from a person under the age of eighteen, is single (divorcees, widows and widowers included) or if the child to be adopted is over eighteen or married. These restrictions do not apply to an application for adoption of a child by a spouse of the parent of the child.

Because of the finality involved in an order for adoption, any person involved, *especially* the child, is advised to seek legal counsel.

3

LEARNING: CHILDREN AND ACCOMMODATION

You have no idea of the destructive effect when a child, such as mine, for example, who has the problem of dyslexia, is called stupid, lazy, a retard, a "spas" and is actually deliberately shut out by the other children. But the attitude of the other children towards her was enhanced by the attitude of the teacher towards her. It enhanced her "differentness". So, what we develop in some of our children is an attitude towards these children whereby they begin to think of themselves as second-class citizens, as different, as strange, and all the other children think of them as strange, as handicapped, as different and as weird. We cause attitudes to develop which are detrimental to both.
—*Reprinted from "Proceedings of the Sub-Committee on Childhood Experiences as Causes of Criminal Behaviour", Senate of Canada, Standing Committee on Health, Welfare and Science, Issue No. 16, Ottawa: June, 1978, representations from the Canadian Association for Children with Learning Disabilities.*

There is no such thing as the natural right of a child to be educated. There is no automatic or inborn compulsion put upon a parent or any person to educate a child. A parent has an obligation under Ontario's *Family Law Reform Act* and Canada's *Criminal Code* to provide necessities of life, but that does not include education. Section 3 of the *Infants Act* provides that rules of equity (essentially, rules of fairness) prevail in all matters relating to the question of a child's custody and education. As one Supreme Court Judge stated: [The court is] "... to act according to what the best interests of the child may require...no matter how the parties got here, and no matter that there may be gaps in the jurisdiction conferred by the Statute".[11]

However, this power to dispense fairness is only available when an issue concerning a child is before the court. This means, practically speaking, that the principles of fairness appear to be of little assistance to a child unless there is a right to appear before a court, a right known as "standing". In the case of education, all rights of the child are derived from the *Education Act, S.O. 1974*, c. 109, and as we shall see, the only clear right is one of accommodation rather than education, and even that right has several infringements. Accommodation means that each tax-paying parent's child is entitled to attend a school and sit in a classroom presided over by a teacher and receive school materials. Nevertheless, in Ontario, the right of equal opportunity to be educated does not exist. The politically expedient policy of stopping short at accommodation offers the tax-payer highly visible results in terms of numbers of bodies and buildings, enabling us all to consider this achievement as an end in itself, comfortably assuming that an effective educative process will automatically ensue. We choose not to open the highly controversial (and highly costly) Pandora's Box of the *quality* of education.

Generally speaking, a child who is entitled to accommodation may attend school without any payment until the last school day in June of the year in which the person attains the age of twenty-one years. The child begins to attend school at the age of six years if his sixth birthday occurs after September 1st, at five years if there is a school in his vicinity that operates a kindergarten, or at four years if the opportunity of a junior kindergarten is available.

The Board of Education

A parent is entitled to damages for failure of the Board of Education to satisfy its duty to provide accommodation and although there may be some discretion as to what is "adequate" accommodation, the duty to provide is absolute. For example, one Board had closed down a school as a result of the Municipality's failure to contribute adequately to the Board's expenditures, an action which deprived the children in the area of schooling for the remainder of the year. The Board argued that compliance with its duty to provide accommodation for the children would be impossible due to lack of funds. On appeal, the court would not accept this as a reason, stating, in part:

> It would be creating a dangerous precedent, under these circumstances to relieve the school board from the absolute and imperative duty to impose upon it by Statute to provide school accommodation to the children within its jurisdiction. To hold otherwise could very well cause public and governmental authorities to disregard prudent limitations upon their expenditures and then permit them to rely upon their own improvidence as an excuse for non-fulfillment of their statutory duty.[12]

While a Board may be under a general obligation to provide accommodation, it is under no obligation to accommodate children in a particular school. The Board has the right to close one or more schools in an area, whether they are of French or English language instruction, so long as one school is available for a child to attend. A Board's move to close a school is not a "statutory power decision" as defined under Ontario's *Statutory Power Procedure Act, 1971* and *Judicial Review Procedure Act, 1971*, and therefore it is not subject to any judicial review. In other words, the question of what kind of school it is, and whether it satisfies the educational needs of the child cannot be reviewed by a court of law.

Education and the Disabled

Obviously, the duty to provide accommodation is far removed from the more essential task of providing adequate instruction. This becomes all too clear in a discussion about children with learning or perceptual handicaps who are "unable to profit" by the instruction available in the schools. Section 34 of the *Education Act* permits the principal of a school to exclude a child from school where that child is unable "...by reason of mental or physical handicap to profit by instruction in an elementary school".

When such discretion is invoked by the principal, he must refer the matter to the appropriate supervisory officer who, in turn, refers it to a local Board. The latter appoints a committee of three persons consisting of the supervisory officer, the principal and a legally qualified medical practitioner where the pupil allegedly has a physical handicap, or a legally qualified psychiatrist where the pupil allegedly has a mental handicap. After studying any existing reports on the child, the committee must then hear the teachers, parents, or guardians of the pupil and any other person who may be able to contribute relevant information. Once the committee has heard all of the evidence, it must notify the Minister of Education as to its decision. If, at a later date, there is a change in the circumstances which warrant the basis for the exclusion decision, a parent has the right to bring the matter back before the Committee for review.

Nevertheless, once the child has been excluded, the Board is under no duty to provide instruction to this child. The Minister of Education has the authority in its complete discretion to establish special education programs for these children, and school boards on their own initiative have the power to establish special education services which then must be conducted pursuant to government regulations covering admissions, progress reports, and class size. Of course, unless appropriate programs are established, the fact that various levels of government have this discretionary power is again one of those examples of adult authority that is of little consolation to the child needing an education. And legislation throughout Canada presently leaves the courts powerless to interfere on behalf of the child.

In contrast, consider the American case in which seven parents of children with learning disabilities argued before a Court in Washington, D.C., that denial of special education programs for their children constituted a violation of the American Bill of Rights, particularly the provision for due process of law. They said that the authorities fell short of due process by failing to ensure that all children had an equal opportunity to be educated in accordance with their needs. Although Canada's constitutional structure does not lend itself to such a legal approach, the words of the court should be interesting to all persons interested in children's education:

> ... The District of Columbia's interest in educating the excluded children clearly must outweigh its interest in preserving its financial resources. If sufficient funds are not available to finance all the services and programs that are needed and desirable in the system, then the available funds must be expended equitably, in such a manner that no child is entirely excluded from publicly supported education consistent with his needs and ability to benefit therefrom. The inadequacies of the District of Columbia's public school system, whether occasioned by insufficient funding or administrative inefficiency, certainly cannot be permitted to bear more heavily on the "exceptional" or handicapped child than on the normal child.[13]

The effect of Section 34 of Ontario's *Education Act* is that children who are unable to profit by instruction in a regular classroom are left to their own devices. In Canada, one child in ten has an emotional or learning disorder, and only Saskatchewan has mandatory legislation concerning the education of children so handicapped. There is presently a bill before the Ontario legislature, the *Education Amendment Act, 1979*, which will ensure that a Board assist any parent or guardian of an excluded child in locating appropriate services and facilities. The Board will also be under a duty to provide its exceptional pupils with adequate education programs. If this Bill is passed, it will be a step welcomed by many children who have been effectively denied an education. As of the date of writing, the Bill has not been passed, and for reasons far removed from individual needs of any child, the Bill is being opposed by many Boards of Education.

A further note: the *Education Act* requires the provision of special classes for "trainable retarded" children. The "trainable retarded" by legislative definition function at a lower level than the "educable retarded" but the former are entitled under the Act to instruction in accordance with their needs and the latter are not.

Many parents have relied in the past upon the *Vocational Rehabilitation Act* to secure an appropriate education for the child who was not profiting from instruction in the usual classroom setting. This act provides for pre-vocational training in its rehabilitation program, and under this aegis many children have been placed in schools outside of Ontario or in private schools in Ontario funded through the Ministry of Community and Social Services, which operates the Vocational Rehabilitative Program. These children thereby receive training to improve their learning faculties as "pre-vocational training".

Moving Through The System

If a child is competent enough to take part in the regular school system, he begins as a pupil in a public elementary school, proceeds through the school's primary and junior divisions, and is then eligible for admission into a secondary school where he will advance to the intermediate and senior divisions. If a child has not been promoted from elementary school, he may still be admitted into a secondary school if the principal of the secondary school is satisfied that the child is competent to undertake the school work. An adverse decision is appealed by seeking a hearing with a local Board which will confirm or overturn the original decision.

A principal also has the power to prevent a pupil from undertaking a certain course of studies when he is of the opinion that the pupil does not display an adequate level of competency. The child then has the option of taking up preparatory course to raise his level of competency or selecting with the approval of the principal an appropriate alternate course. If the pupil is under the age of eighteen years, the consent of a parent or guardian has to be obtained before he engages in an alternative program. There is *no* appeal from this decision, one which may determine the child's stream of studies and, very probably, his vocation in life.

In the microsociety of the school there exists a hierarchy comprised of the Board, the principal, the teachers and the students. The fact that a student's rights and freedoms are circumscribed more stringently in the school quarters than on the city streets can be rationalized as being necessary for the achievement of society's primary objective for young people: education. When, in the name of efficiency, do we stifle the process of learning by smothering spontaneity, curiosity and adventure? When do we cross the threshold of protecting our children through the *Education Act* and begin to threaten his civil liberties?

Religion, Censorship and Privacy

Religious exercises are held daily in each classroom. However, if a parent or guardian sends written notice to the teacher requiring his child's exclusion for religious reasons, the request will be honoured. Interestingly enough, there is no provision for a pupil's exemption from patriotic exercises. (The opening of closing exercises of each school day should include *O Canada* and may include *God Save the Queen*.) Nevertheless, in one Ontario case, the Court held that "patriotic exercises" may have a religious significance and consequently fall within the religious instruction exemption.

Censorship is utilized widely in our schools and has recently been discovered by the media as a contentious issue, especially in light of one Board's banning of Margaret Laurence's books. All textbooks used in a school must be sanctioned by the local board, thereby creating varying standards among the different jurisdictions which theoretically reflect the varying morals of each community. Censorship decision-making becomes even more decentralized where, in the case of the distribution of literature on school property, each principal is entrusted with discretionary power.

One issue that I am often questioned about concerns the privacy of the child's school locker. A pupil's locker belongs to him only in the sense that he has a license to use it. The locker is property belonging to the Board. The principal is required by the regulations to inspect the school premises regularly and instruct pupils in the care of the school premises. These sections give the principal the necessary degree of discretion to search a student's locker, particularly in an emergency situation, or, alternatively, to request that a student open his locker so that it may be checked. If a student refuses, then he may be showing "persistent opposition to authority" and be subject to suspension proceedings.

At best, a pupil who is concerned about the privacy of his personal property within the school locker should check with the Board policy in advance. Some Boards direct that a principal is not to open a student's locker unless there is an emergency, or unless he has the consent of the pupil or his parents. Some Boards will require the school principal to ensure that the pupil has the opportunity to nominate a teacher as a witness if a locker is to be opened on a day where it is known the pupil will be absent. Police officers do have the right to search school lockers at *any time* under the *Narcotics Control Act*, and under the *Food and Drug Act* if they have reasonable grounds to suspect illegal possession of an item, but the school official is definitely not that police officer. His authority derives solely from the *Education Act* as discussed above.

Privacy is also an issue with respect to the student's records. A "pupil record" is established and maintained by the principal of a school in accordance with the education for each student. It consists of a record folder, the pupil's achievement forms, documents, photographs, information in writing inserted in the record folder with the approval of the principal and an index card.

It is important to note that the "record" exists for the information and use of supervisory officers, the principal and teachers of the school, for the improvement of instruction of the pupil, and is not to be made available to any other person. Nor is it admissible in evidence for any purpose in any trial, inquest, inquiry, examination, hearing or other proceeding except to prove the establishment, maintenance, retention or transfer of the record unless there has first been written permission of the parent or guardian — or, when the pupil is eighteen years or more, written permission of the pupil.

A student, and, if a child (under eighteen years), his parent or guardian, is entitled to examine the record. The Act provides the parent with remedies if information is inaccurately recorded or is "not conducive to the improvement of instruction of the pupil". The parent may ask the principal to correct or remove items from the record; if the principal refuses, the parent may involve a supervisory officer. He then may either require the principal to comply or cause a hearing to be held to settle the issue.

Finally, information in the record is strictly confidential and no person is to communicate its contents to any other person except as may be required in the performance of his duties, or in the case of written consent of the student, or parent if the student is a minor. The contents will also be made available to the student if eighteen years of age, or otherwise to the parent if it is for the purpose of enrolling in an educational institution outside of Ontario. Further rules governing the transfer of records can be found in the Regulations to the *Education Act*.

Discipline

Conduct which otherwise might constitute assault is an accepted part of parent-child dynamics at common law, and is also applicable to the teacher/student relationship. It is said that the parent, by sending his child to school, delegates his disciplinary rights to the teacher. S. 43 of the *Criminal Code* gives statutory sanction to this principle. Moreover, because the teacher's power is seen as necessary for maintaining order in the classroom, and not simply for meting out parental punishment, the teacher is empowered to exercise necessary discipline, even over the objections of the parent. Such disciplinary powers entrusted to the teacher have been held to extend even outside the school "... if the effects of the act ... reach within the school room during school hours [and] are detrimental to good order and the best interests of pupils ..."

Although S. 43 of the *Criminal Code* sanctions reasonable corporal punishment by all parents and teachers, each Board sets up its own policies. For example, the Toronto Board of Education has forbidden all forms of corporal punishment, while the North York Board of Education has limited the means of corporal punishment to strapping. One Magistrate wrote, in 1933: "... He was beaten at school, the implication, of course, being that the beating made him the fine fellow he is".[14] With respect to the learned Magistrate, until the welcomed day when all corporal punishment is abolished, we must rely on various guidelines extracted from case law. These guidelines set out just what is "reasonable" punishment — not by my standards, mind you, just by the courts'.

As examples, the courts have considered temporary marks on a child's skin, or discolouration of the skin lasting for a few days as being reasonable; a teacher pulling a child out of his desk, shoving him along the aisle — which resulted in the pupil falling and hitting his head on the floor — reasonable! Or, there is the case of a teacher tripping a pupil, sitting on him, and, with a ruler, hitting him on his shoulders and the backs of his hands causing bruises and welts, all of which was considered reasonable.

It took the case of a child sustaining a chronic condition of mastitis as a result of strapping and blows on her breast for the court finally to recognize that force exercised by a teacher can be *un*reasonable. Even here, the courts were no comfort to the child when it suggested that the teacher's use of force would have been reasonable if the child's wrists had been held — to confine any blows from the strap to the palm of her hand, "as they should be". In other cases, force has been held "unreason-able" when there is a risk of permanent injury. As one court noted:

> . . . [To] hit a child on the spine with a hard object such as a ruler would, in my opinion, be unjustified, no matter what his offence. Also, though to a lesser degree, to discipline a nine year old child and one of six years by banging their knuckles on the corner of the desk is injurious and may be unjustified. The covering over the bones on the back of the hands is very thin and the risk of permanent injury is correspondingly greater.[15]

Can we really talk about "reasonable" and "unreasonable" force when those concerned are flesh-and-blood children, our children?

It would surely be simpler if we abolished corporal punish-ment altogether, placing the onus for justification on teachers or principals if they should have to resort to force. It would also make more sense, if we are actually concerned with discipline. Every time a child is hit at school, it is only a lesson to him and every witness that hitting another person is acceptable conduct in our society. Moreover, retaining corporal punishment in the schools reinforces the prejudices of some parents, whose stand-ards of home punishment can amount to child abuse.

When this issue arises in lectures, high school teachers often jump to their feet with horror stories about student brutality. We are told that a fourteen-year-old kid is really an adult, and when he gets violent, commando tactics are needed. Those who don't see how dangerous our children have become are simply naive, we are told: they have learned gangster tactics from television and are past masters in holding up class proce-dures and terrorizing the halls. Fed on vitamins and junk food, these kids are *big*, too; you need a chair and a whip just to get the roll called.

Well, maybe, in a few instances, but it's worth noting that most cases involving corporal punishment come from the primary schools, and it's hard to believe that the kids there are bigger and meaner than the teachers. What kind of teacher is it who can't handle, say, a fifth grader without causing flesh wounds? Teachers using the strap, like parents dragging out the wooden paddle or leather belt, are only carrying on the good old Canadian tradition, our heritage from the nightmare of the 19th century British public school system.

Corporal punishment cannot be justified in the elementary school, or the secondary school. There is a major distinction between sanctioning the use of force, the intentional infliction of pain as discipline, and the dragging — if all else fails — of a seventeen-year-old from the classroom. If ever a situation gets so tense that only violence can resolve it, then surely the child needs special additional resources for his learning. And a good blow on the head, a whop on the back, or a bracing strap of the knuckles are not resources.

Section 22 of the *Education Act* provides the principal with the authority to suspend a pupil for a period not in excess of a period established by the Board. Children can be suspended for persistent truancy, persistent opposition to authority, habitual neglect of duty, the wilful destruction of school property, the use of profane or improper language or conduct injurious to the moral tone of the school, or to the physical and mental well-being of others in the school. In short, the child can be suspended for almost anything. A suspension of a child by the principal will usually result in a temporary absence from the school for a fixed period.

Expulsion, on the other hand, is an additional disciplinary power which can be exercised only by a Board decision, and which may result in an indefinite absence from all schools under the Board's jurisdiction. A Board may expel a pupil from its schools if the pupil's conduct "is so refractory that his presence is injurious to others". If expulsion is recommended by the principal and a supervisory officer, the parents are to be notified in writing and have the right to make representation at a hearing to be conducted by the Board.

In the case of either a suspension or an expulsion, it is the parents, not the student, who will make submissions concerning action, unless the child is of the age of eighteen years. That is, though it is the student's rights which are to be affected, he is not a party to the proceedings. Unfortunately, parents can have a tendency to side with the educational authorities in approaching the hearing as an opportunity to investigate their child's unacceptable conduct for themselves. However, many Boards will allow the child to have representation, though it is not expressly provided for in the Act. Children should make such a request whenever there is a possibility that they will be suspended or expelled from a school.

Leaving School

Whether it was to legitimize the number of truants or to provide a more comprehensive education, the legislature has codified a policy of early school-leaving for students fourteen years of age or more. On application, they may be excused from full-time or part-time attendance as part of an out-of-school training program. In order to qualify for early school-leaving, the parents of the child submit an application in writing, outlining why he or she considers that the child should be excused from attendance at school. The application requires information as to the possible provision of alternative education programs. The lack of such information is not fatal to its processing, although it lends more effective support to the submission.

As an example, the application might set out that the child finds no interest in school, and desires an opportunity to work. The application would be enhanced if the child could state that he has contacted various possible employers, or better still, that he has an opportunity to become involved in a training program. An application for early school-leaving can only be submitted by a parent or guardian, offering the fourteen-year-old no remedy if his parents are in opposition to the plan.

An early school-leaving committee reviews the application and sets up a program for the child, usually one which involves part-time school attendance (note that any program for employment must overcome the hurdles imposed by all the various statutes which exist in Ontario concerning the employment of children: see Chapter 4). Once a program has been agreed upon by the parent and the Committee, the pupil is excused from attendance only so long as he conforms to the program and he maintains the status of a "pupil", thus remaining under the supervision of the school authorities. In fact, failure to comply with the program without sufficient reason makes both the child and the parents subject to prosecution on the basis of the pupil's unlawful attendance. An early school-leaving program does not mean that the child is not attending school. It simply means that the child's attendance is defined differently from that of the child who sits day after day in the classroom.

Perhaps the most expedient and popular way of dealing with children who are not making it in the public education system is use of the truancy offence or, in present-day jargon, "unlawful absence from school". S. 20(5) of the *Education Act* directs the parent or guardian to cause the child of six to sixteen years to attend school, and failure to do so constitutes an offence unless the child is legally excused. More often than not, the person who is brought to court is the child and not the parent or guardian. S. (29)5 describes the offence as being "...habitually absent from school" and any child who is so absent, is guilty of an offence and can be dealt with by the court as if he had been adjudged a juvenile delinquent. "Habitually" in practice requires a pattern of absenteeism. Gone are the days when one day hooky results in a charge of truancy.

The *Education Act* appears to categorize truancy as a summary offence, using the *Juvenile Delinquents Act* only with respect to disposition. However, S. 39 of the *Juvenile Delinquents Act* gives the alternative of proceeding by way of Provincial Statute without adjudication of juvenile delinquency if in the best interests of the child and if the child has not committed an indictable offence according to the *Criminal Code*. Staying away from school is not an indictable offence. Therefore, the truant child could be proceeded against in this way rather than engaging the more serious delinquency machinery. Surely, it was not the intention of the *Education Act* in establishing the offence to lump a truant child with a child who has been charged with break and enter. Is it really the desire of the Legislature to burden a child with a criminal record for want of attendance at school? Even the *Child Welfare Act* offers a more sensible route than a finding of delinquency. That Act includes as one of the grounds for a child to be found "in need of protection", "unlawful absence from school". Unfortunately, most courts in Ontario continue to apply the *Juvenile Delinquents Act* to truancy situations.

The community and the police deal differently with kids who are branded "juvenile delinquents" than they do with children who are subject to proceedings under the *Child Welfare Act* or *Education Act*. In general, the police do not ponder the reasons underlying the label "delinquent" and will assume that the child committed a crime. Furthermore, the Juvenile Court possesses an inordinate degree of power over a truant, considering the mildness of his offence. Since the child is a delinquent, he can be brought back to court at any time until he is twenty-one, and the court can throw him into training school — and all because the kid got bored in class. For these reasons, raise the roof if the *Juvenile Delinquents Act* is used with your child when truancy is the issue.

A child may be lawfully absent from school, if his absence can be justified by any of the following reasons:

(a) The child is receiving satisfactory instruction at home or elsewhere;

(b) The child is sick;

(c) The child cannot get to school because the school is too far away from his home and the Board of Education is not providing transportation. Specifically, he is not forced to go to school where there is no transportation provided by the Board, and the school is not within one mile of his home if he is under seven years; two miles from his home if he is over six years and under ten years; or three miles from his home if he is under sixteen;

(d) The child has already received a secondary school graduation diploma or has completed a course that gives him an equivalent standing as assessed by the Board;

(e) The child is absent because he is receiving music instruction, and his absence does not exceed one-half day in a week. Just what is music instruction is a decision the family makes without any discretion left to the Minister of Education;

(f) The child is absent on a day regarded as a Holy Day by the church of the family's religion. Here too, just what is a Holy Day is a decision for the family and the Minister of Education has no discretion with respect to religious days;

(g) If the child is suspended, expelled or excluded from attendance, then the Act tells us that he has a "legal" excuse for not attending; and

(h) The child is legally absent or excused by way of enrollment in the early school leaving program, as an example.

The enforcement of school attendance in the Province is accomplished through the authority of a Provincial School Attendance Counsellor appointed by the Cabinet with subordinates appointed by each Board. The School Attendance Counsellor is the new euphemistic title for the dreaded "truant officer". School Attendance Officers are to inquire into every case of failure to attend school in their knowledge, and if there's no legal excuse, they are to give written warning of the consequences both to the parent and the child and to exhort them to cause attendance forthwith. The warning must, at the same time, advise the parent or guardian of their right to defend or explain their child's alleged unlawful absence from school by appearing before a Committee appointed by the Board. The Committee, after conducting a hearing, will determine whether the parent's explanation is satisfactory. One parent argued, for example, that her child attending at an independent "free school" received satisfactory instruction. Upon investigation, the explanation satisfied the Committee and the child was legally excused. In other words, the "legal excuse" provision provides for various defences to a charge of truancy and opens the way to some extent, to legitimate alternative forms of education as competition to the public school system.

Note that no provision exists within the Act to allow a child, who may be in conflict with his parents, to demand an inquiry to determine the validity of *his* excuse, a feature which we noted in discussions on suspension and expulsion. Accordingly, unless the parent supports the child in his absence from school, the above-mentioned investigative process would not be carried out. The School Attendance Officer may simply, pursuant to the Act, institute legal action through a charge against the child in Juvenile Court for unlawful absence from school. Fortunately, the Act allows the court to refer the matter back to the Provincial School Attendance Officer for inquiry if it appears to the judge that there may be a legal excuse. In this way, the court may effectively act on behalf of the child, insuring that he be given the same rights as his parents to be heard within the education, rather than the court system.

A special case of truancy involves the Native child. The Federal Government has exclusive jurisdiction over the education of Indian children as defined under Canada's *Indian Act*, and exercises this power through the Ministry for Northern and Indian Affairs. There is quite a difference, however, if you are a child accused of truancy under the *Indian Act* or a child similarly accused under the *Education Act*.

For example, a truant officer under the *Indian Act* may take into custody any Native child he reasonably believes is unlawfully absent from school and convey the child to school "using as much force as the circumstances require". The latitude allowed in the officer's application of force under the *Indian Act* is absent in the *Education Act*, where a School

Attendance Counsellor may not enter a dwelling place to take a child to school without a warrant. Furthermore, the truant officer, under Ontario's *Education Act* may not convey the child anywhere unless requested to do so by the principal or parent. Unlike the *Education Act*, a warrant or a request by a parent or principal does not seem to be necessary. Indeed, under Canada's *Indian Act*, the truant officer has all the powers of a peace officer and may enter any place where he believes, on reasonable grounds, that there are Native children unlawfully absent from school.

A further difference is the fact that a Native child who refuses or fails to attend school (or is expelled or suspended) will be deemed a juvenile delinquent within the meaning of the *Juvenile Delinquents Act*. To be clear, that means that the mere allegation by a truant officer that a Native child refuses or fails to attend school is all that is necessary for a finding of juvenile delinquency. On the other hand, such an allegation under the *Education Act* must be tested in a court of law where a judge will determine whether there is a just excuse for the non-Indian child's absence.

In fact, the only reason the Indian child appears in court is to find out his sentence upon being deemed a delinquent. Also, under the *Indian Act*, an Indian child is not required to attend school if there is insufficient accommodation. Such an excuse for absence from school does not exist under the *Education Act* where, as we have seen, there is a strict duty upon the Board of Education to provide accommodation for all children who live in their jurisdiction. The Native child is exposed to a system whose governing statutes seem to sanction the very denial of the right to accommodation: entrenched laws smacking of discrimination.

4

CHILDREN:
THE IMPOTENT CITIZENS

Newspaper publishers and an awful lot of parents think that having a paper route is "good for a kid". It teaches him to handle the basic fundamentals of our free enterprise system. But there is another side to that coin. The *fifth estate* investigated the employment and business practices of Canadian newspaper publishers, and we have come to the conclusion that the kids are exploited. There are no fringe benefits. The hours are long and hard. The money just isn't consistent with the size of bundles that these kids have to carry, or the weather in which they have to work. They distribute free advertising material from which the publishers make an awful lot of money. We asked Toronto *Star* publisher Beland Honderich if his Legal Department had ever considered the possibility that the carriers are employees.

"I don't think the question has ever been raised here, to my knowledge. I know there has been discussions about it in the newspaper industry generally, but it has never been a problem. I have never paid any particular attention to that precise point you are raising".

—*Excerpt from the transcript of CBC's the* fifth estate, *February, 1978.*

In the event a child can find work, he has the right to retain his wages in the face of any parental claims. The Catch-22 is that by working, he very likely will be breaking one of the many laws enacted to protect him and making himself liable to a juvenile delinquency charge.

Ontario's *Education Act* requires everyone up to the age of sixteen to attend school unless legally excused, and employment itself isn't one of these legal exceptions. There is nothing in the *Education Act* that prevents the child from working outside of school hours, on a weekend, or on school holidays. But even here there are limitations placed on what a minor may or may not do.

According to the *Industrial Safety Act*, a child under the age of sixteen years may not be employed in a factory or place where manufacturing, assembling, preparing, inspecting, finishing, or cleaning of goods or products is carried on. Neither can a child work in a construction project, according to the same Act, or, thanks to the *Loggers' Safety Act* and the *Mining Act* respectively, in a logging camp or around a mine or plant. A child under the age of sixteen years cannot supervise the riding of horses pursuant to the *Riding Horse Establishment Act* or obtain a license under the *Game and Fish Act*. He cannot engage in a trade or occupation in a place to which the public has access between 9 o'clock in the evening and 6 o'clock in the morning of the following day. Neither can he be involved in any form of entertainment for profit during the same hours unless the child has the permission of the Children's Aid Society. All these limitations on his ability to work are a result of Ontario's *Child Welfare Act*, which may be imposing values of Oliver Twist's England upon children of today in Canada. These Statutes represent some of the ways in which the law interferes with the child's ability to do something other than go to school and grow up a "good boy" or "nice girl".

The Working Child

If the child decides to be self-employed, which is one way of overcoming the Statutory obstacles for employment, he faces the hurdle of his legal incapacity to make a contract, certainly an essential part of any business. To protect children from their lack of knowledge and experience, contract law establishes special rules for those under the age of majority, which in Ontario, is eighteen years. While there are certain exceptions, contracts entered into by children are "voidable", meaning:

(a) valid and binding upon the child unless he repudiates them before or within a reasonable time after he reaches the age of eighteen years, or

(b) not binding upon the child unless he specifically ratifies them when he reaches the age of eighteen years.

The mechanism of "voidability" allows the child to contract with an adult but insures that there is no permanent or irrevocable liability for the child until he is an adult, at which time he will be deemed to understand the consequences of entering into a contract which can be legally avoided by the minor party at some future date.

There are some exceptions to this general rule that are worth consideration. Where a contract is clearly detrimental to the interests of the child, a judge will find it is void from the outset if the adult tries to enforce its provisions in court. This means that the contract is not even subject to possible validation through ratification, nor are its terms enforceable until repudiated. In one case, a minor entered a contract for the purchase of land which contained a severe forfeiture clause in the event that payments were in default. In finding it prejudicial to the child's interests, the court held the contract to be void and therefore invalid from the outset. Accordingly, the child was entitled to recover any payments made under the terms of the contract.

On the other hand, those contracts which provide "necessaries" are presumed to be binding upon the child if the terms are to his benefit. "Necessaries" have been held to include those things which the child requires for his living, health and education and anything ancillary thereto. The term "necessaries" is a relative expression to be construed in light of the child's age, needs and standard of living. Because the law considers that a child does not have sufficient maturity to carry on a trade or business, the courts have held that services supplied to the child in the course of his training or business, while necessary for carrying on the trade or business, are not considered to be a "necessary" to the child. Therefore, a contract for the purpose of supplying goods or services to a child's business, is not binding upon the child. Somewhat inhibiting to the minor entrepreneur, to say the least.

Contracts of service or employment, if beneficial to the child, are also presumed to be binding upon him. In determining whether the contract is for the benefit of the child, the court will compare the specific terms to those generally used by employers in that field, and will assess its propensity to protect the child, to insure secure employment and to provide sufficient remuneration for self-maintenance and fair compensation. The contract must be clearly beneficial to the child, and the onus will be on the employer to demonstrate this fact. In light of this judicial approach, it would seem that the newspaper carriers in advancing their case before the court would find firm legal ground for their position.

A child's interest in any land cannot be transferred without following procedures set out in Ontario's *Infants Act*, and failure to comply with those procedures will render any transaction void. There are specific rules to protect a child's interest in any property. For example, a child is often the beneficiary of his parent's estate under a will, or pursuant to the *Succession Law Reform Act* when there is no will. In these instances, the Ontario reader is advised to consult the office of the Official Guardian, whose mailing address in Toronto is 180 Dundas Street West, 6th Floor, Toronto, Ontario, M5E 1E4. (The overall intent of these requirements is to insure that the short and long-term financial welfare of the child is not jeopardized by adult dealings.)

As an illustration of the Official Guardian's involvement, you may recall the case of the child who won on a lottery ticket but was not allowed to spend any of the money without government supervision. The Official Guardian became involved because Ontario's *Trustee Act* provides that when any person is entitled to money, the person to whom the money is entitled — in this, a lottery scheme — may pay the money into the Supreme Court of Ontario to the credit of the child instead of paying it to the child directly. Payment into the Supreme Court of Ontario represents a complete discharge of the payor's liability, protecting him in the lottery scheme as a whole against possible repercussion stemming from the minority status of the beneficiary. On paying into court, the payor must also provide an affidavit setting out the facts entitling the child to the money, the child's birth date, name and address, and the name and address of the persons with whom the child resides.

Ontario's *Apprenticeship and Tradesmen's Qualification Act* establishes an "apprentice" program for persons who are at least sixteen years of age, and who have entered into a contract in which they are to receive, from or through their employer, training and instruction in a specified trade. The contract of apprenticeship must be for a period of at least two years, according to the prescribed form, and signed by the employer, by the person to be apprenticed and, if the person to be apprenticed is under eighteen years of age, by his parent or guardian. If neither the parent or the guardian is willing to sign, or is incapable of signing, a Judge of the County or District Court in which the employer carries on business may, upon application, dispense with their signature. Finally, any contract of apprenticeship must be approved by the Director of the program. If the contract satisfies these apprenticeship parameters, it is not subject to the usual limitations on a minor's capacity to contract. Some contracts of apprenticeship include alignment and brake mechanic, auto body repairer, carpenter, plumber, or brick stone mason.

A Child's Rights

Canadian law is enlightened in its insistence on the welfare of the child as the centre of concern in all matters of employment, law-breaking, custody and support. And yet, for those who work with kids, or know kids, or even read about kids in the newspapers, it becomes clear that the child's welfare is somehow the first thing to vanish away when it comes to legal hassles among parents, money rights, or mere common-sense fair treatment from the adult world. If the law manages to protect children from certain obvious wrongs, it is also there to restrict the child from the fullest involvement in everyday life. If you know a child, read him a list of the things he or she cannot do in our society, and see if the child thinks it all makes sense. For example:

You cannot make a will unless you are eighteen years of age... You cannot vote and you cannot hold office in the Provincial Legislative assembly or Parliament unless you are eighteen... You cannot drive a car or snowmobile until you are sixteen... You cannot drink or be sold liquor until you are nineteen... You cannot smoke a cigarette until you are eighteen... You cannot be a director of your company until you are eighteen, although you might be an officer of the corporation except for the President... You cannot go to a movie after the hour of 7:30 p.m. on any day, or during school days, unless you are twelve years of age and accompanied by a person over the age of sixteen, and, of course, you have to wait until you reach eighteen years until you see any film classified as "restricted"... You have to put up with your name because you cannot change it until you are at least eighteen years of age under Ontario's *Change of Name Act*... You cannot get legally married, according to Ontario's *Marriage Act* if you are under the age of sixteen, and if you are sixteen or seventeen, you can only get married if you have a consent in writing of both parents. (If your parents won't give you their consent, or if they are not available, you, in your own right, can make an application to a Judge of the Provincial or County Court and he can dispense with the required consent)... You cannot get life insurance until you are sixteen, and even if you do, and you are under eighteen, obtaining life insurance is considered not to be a necessary expenditure by the courts who restrict your ability to borrow money in order to have insurance... And, YOU CANNOT SEEK HELP IF YOU ARE DISCRIMINATED AGAINST BECAUSE YOU ARE A CHILD. Discrimination on the basis of age in Ontario's Human Rights Code refers only to persons forty years and more, or less than sixty-five years.

When, in spite of everything, a child does participate in "adult" activities and happens to cause harm to other persons or to property, questions often arise concerning the extent of his liability. One American judgment, in considering the dilemma, stated:

> We agree that minors are entitled to be judged by standards commensurate with their age, experience and wisdom when engaged in activities appropriate to their age, experience and wisdom. Hence, when children are walking, running, playing with toys, playing ball, operating bicycles, sliding or engaged in other child's activities, their conduct should be judged by the rule of what is reasonable conduct under the circumstances among which are the age, experience, and stage of mental development of the minor involved. However, the question is raised by the defendant in this case whether the standard of care applied to minors in such cases should prevail when the minor is engaged in activities normally undertaken by adults ... We are of the opinion that to apply to minors a more lenient standard in the operation of motor vehicles, whether an automobile or motorcycle, than that applied to adults, is unrealistic, contrary to the express legislative policy and contrary to public safety.[16]

If a child is found to be negligent, he can be sued for his wrongful act and is not protected as in contract law. The only exceptions to his liability might occur when a child has wrongfully injured a person, but is so young that the courts cannot construe any intention on the child's part to commit such an act. For example, when a three-year-old child dragged a baby from its pram, the child was found not to be liable for the wrongful act of battery since the intention to cause harm to another person was obviously lacking. Yet, a five-year-old who had intended to slash his friend with a razor was found liable: while not understanding the gravity of his action, this child nevertheless had the intention to cause harm.

Liability to a child who has been harmed is determined, as in contract law, by special rules stemming from the uniqueness of childhood. "Occupier's liability" is the phrase used to describe a land-owner's responsibility to keep visitors and even trespassers relatively free from harm. The responsibility of the landowner varies in degree: trespassers, for example, enter with a greater risk than a person invited onto the property, or a person paying rent for being on the property. Yet the courts have always expected a higher standard of care from an occupier when trespass involves a wandering child; gravel pits, ponds and wild places are attractive to children, who are not expected to have a broad understanding of the law. These days, the courts simply ask, "What are reasonable precautions in the circumstances?"

Let's look at one case in which several children had come onto a property, played among inflammable barrels, and ended up in the hospital with severe burn injuries. The children, through their parents, sued the company that owned the property and ran the business there. The court held:

> The injury having occurred, we ask ourselves whether or not this sort of injury was foreseeable on the part of the occupier, and whether, if it was foreseeable, he safeguarded against it. We must ask ourselves whether the precautions taken by the occupier to guard against the risk of injury were reasonable considering the use that he knew, or should have known, would be made of the property by persons coming on the property without permission. An occupier is not required to take extra extravagant precautions. He must match the precaution to risk. Unfortunately, too often the occupier shelters behind a policy of insurance rather than a chain-link fence . . . I have no doubt that the damage and injury were foreseeable. The occupier knew of the inflammable and explosive nature of the contents of the stored barrels, and should have foreseen the danger of injury. Furthermore in

my view, the precautions were inadequate. The only pre-
caution was the direction to the employees to tighten the
bungs with a bung wrench and store the barrels topped to
the wall. It was foreseeable that these instructions would
not be strictly followed. It was foreseeable that children
would play around barrels and would try to investigate
the contents.[17]

A simple sign warning people not to trespass would not obviate
the company's liability in the above case. All children cannot
read or understand; some children simply haven't learned to
obey three-syllable words.

It seems clear that children do not support themselves.
They are expected to attend school on a full-time basis, and
their parents are expected to shoulder their living expenses for
the first sixteen to eighteen years of their life. Under Ontario's
Family Law Reform Act, 1978, every parent has an obligation,
to the extent that he or she is capable, to provide support in
accordance with the child's needs until he reaches the age of
eighteen years (or sixteen years if the child withdraws voluntar-
ily from his parents' control). "Need" is a relative term,
although necessities of life, as a bottom-line test, have been
held by the courts to include medical treatment, articles of
clothing, shelter, household equipment, education and training for a trade.

Who Supports The Kids?

Where parties are involved in a divorce under Canada's
Divorce Act, the question of support will arise for those children under the age of sixteen—and over sixteen, if the child, as a
result of being ill, disabled, or for whatever cause, is unable to
withdraw himself from his parents' charge and provide himself
with the necessaries of life. The courts liberally interpret this
latter status, not restricting it to an illness or disability, but

including the child's pursuit of an education. However, in one case in which a "child" had reached the age of twenty-one years and was attending university, the court held that the word "child" under the *Divorce Act* should be read in its ordinary sense and no obligation of support should be owed to a healthy, able-bodied son or daughter, twenty-one years of age and over, who decides to extend his educational career indefinitely, particularly where the evidence shows that the child has a capacity to earn a sufficient amount of money to complete his course.

For the purpose of either Ontario's *Family Law Reform Act, 1978* or Canada's *Divorce Act*, the definition of "child" is not restricted to a biological relationship, or, in the case of the Ontario Act, to persons who are born to parents lawfully married. The *Divorce Act* defines a child to whom an obligation of support is owed as "any person to whom the husband and wife stand *in loco parentis* (in place of the parent) and any person of whom either the husband or the wife is the parent and to whom the other of them stands *in loco parentis*." For example, a divorced mother remarries and for two years lives with a second husband who assumes the role of father to her children. It is likely, that the second husband stands *in loco parentis* to his wife's children and is therefore liable to contribute to support. The court will use these guidelines:

(1) Did the second husband provide a large part of the financial support necessary for the child's maintenance?

(2) Did he intend to step into the father's shoes?

(3) Was the relationship between the wife's second husband and her children a continuing one, with the idea of permanency?

(4) If the children were living with and supported by their own father, the mother's first husband, has the second husband nevertheless essentially replaced the "parental role" of the first husband?

(5) Has the person, at the time which the action comes to the court, continued to stand *in loco parentis*?

Ontario's *Family Law Reform Act* seems more extensive

than the *Divorce Act* in its definition of "child" and "parent". A child may be "born within or outside of marriage, and includes a person whom the parent has demonstrated a settled intention to treat as a child of his or her family, but does not include a child placed in a foster home for consideration by a person having lawful custody". "Parent" is defined as "the father or mother of a child, and includes a person who has demonstrated a settled intention to treat a child as a child of his or her family, but does not include a person in whose home a child was placed as a foster child for a consideration by a person having lawful custody".

The *Divorce Act* standard of *in loco parentis* requires a more subjective test than the standard of "demonstrating a settled intention to treat the child as a member of the family" under the Provincial *Family Law Reform Act, 1978*. By the latter's wording, the courts should look at the family dynamics, including the child's *de facto* provision as well as the adult's intentions. Whether that adult stands *in loco parentis*, on the other hand, according to the *Divorce Act*, depends to a significant extent, on whether he or she intends to do so. In cases of marital breakdown, a child might find himself without support, because his parents are seeking a divorce under Canada's *Divorce Act*; another child may get support because the parents only want relief arising from separation under the *Family Law Reform Act*. A stepfather who had lived with a child for two years and had assumed some financial responsibility for his upbringing might successfully raise a defence that he had never intended to act as the child's parent concerning full financial responsibility. However, if the action were under the *Family Law Reform Act*, his defence would stand less chance if it was decided that there was a parent-child relationship in the home. There is really no reason why one child should suffer from lack of support simply because his parents are in the process of a divorce, thereby necessitating the use of the Federal *Divorce Act* instead of the Provincial *Family Law Reform Act*. The issue is the same: child support. Here we go again, one of those adult anomalies that are of little consolation to the child.

Legitimacy

One important feature of the Provincial definition is the specific end to any distinction between children born in and outside of marriage. Ontario's *Children's Law Reform Act, 1977* abolished the status of "illegitimacy", equalizing the legal rights of all children in the province — and high time, given the growing number of common law relationships in North American society. The stigma of bastardy is a prime example of adult prejudices getting in the way of a fair deal for children. At common law, a child born outside marriage has long been regarded as a "son of nobody", with no rights or obligations attached to the biological relationship. The child could not expect to inherit or receive support from his father or mother, and neither parent had a right to custody or guardianship of the illegitimate child. Gradually, the harshness of the law was alleviated by a piecemeal approach to reform — making the father, for example, financially liable for the support of the child. Some Statutes, such as Ontario's *Workmen's Compensation Act* did include the illegitimate child in its definition of a "member of the family".

Section 1 of the *Children's Law Reform Act* clearly states that a person is a child of his or her parents, and the status of a child is unaffected by the marital status of the parents. Unless there is a clear statement that specifically distinguishes the "illegitimate child", a reference to "child" in an existing will, legal document, Act or Regulation means *all* children, whether or not their parents are married. If, however, a millionaire executed a will prior to March 31, 1978, the date the *Children's Law Reform Act* was proclaimed, and in that will left $200,000 to each of his five children and their children in the event that any of his own children predecease him, but *not* any grandchildren born from unwed parents, then the law of "bastardy" prevails, and the illegitimate child receives nothing. Apparently, the law considers the value of our last respects to the wishes of the dying (who, after all, in this situation, knew nothing of such liberal thoughts) to be more important than the bastard child. Of some consolation is the fact that after March 31st, 1978, it doesn't matter what the testator says in his will. *All* the kids share, however they come into this world.

Although there is theoretically no difference in child-support considerations between those born in and those born outside of marriage, acknowledgment or a finding of biological parentage is a prerequisite in cases in which the mother is not married to the father. Once the determination is made, that parent will incur the responsibility of all parents with respect to their children. The court has the power to grant leave to obtain blood tests of all persons who are suspected of being the father or mother of the child. While the court may not compel a party to submit to blood tests, any refusal to do so allows the judge to draw an adverse inference against that party.

In a recent Ontario proceeding, leave was granted to conduct tests when the facts showed that one of two men could have been the father and a haematologist stated that analyses of blood samples could determine the identity. This is an important procedure, because as long as there are two possible fathers and the judge can't find either to be the father in fact, neither is responsible for supporting the child! Reform legislation in one Province of Canada is, at least, considering that the court could find two or more possible fathers financially responsible for the support of the child and apportion the amount of liability amongst them.

Seeking a judicial determination of parentage is not necessary in any of the following situations:

(1) The alleged father is married to the mother of the child at the time of the birth of the child;

(2) The alleged father was married to the mother of the child by a marriage that was terminated by death or a judgment of nullity or divorce (Decree Absolute) within 300 days before the birth of the child;

(3) The alleged father married the mother of the child after the birth, and acknowledges that he is the natural father;

(4) The alleged father was cohabiting with the mother of

the child in a relationship of some permanence at the time of the birth of the child, or the child is born 300 days after they cease to cohabit;

(5) The alleged father and mother of the child have filed a statutory declaration under the *Vital Statistics Act* acknowledging their parentage of the child;

(6) The alleged father has been found or recognized in his lifetime by another court to be the father of the child.

If any one of these circumstances exist, there is a presumption that the male is the father of the child, and he is to be recognized as such, unless it can be proven on a balance of probabilities that, in spite of all the circumstances, he isn't. Unfortunately for the child, when two or more of these circumstances implicate more than one man, no presumption of parentage can be made, and the finding will be determined without the presumption. The application can be made by any person "having an interest", meaning the child, but including as well the custodial parent or individual caring for the child. The application must be made while the child and the alleged parent are alive; however, once made, an order for support can be pending upon the determined parent's estate.

Before the *Family Law Reform Act, 1978*, the mother's testimony needed corroboration by a third party or through independent evidence before a finding could be made. Under the new legislation, corroboration is no longer a prerequisite, although evidence from a third party or a "third party situation" is certainly desirable in proving parentage. A mother wishing to prove that someone is the father of a child won't get far if all she can present to the court is her word (invariably against *his* word). Evidence to corroborate or substantiate her word might include the alleged father's encouragement that she have an abortion, or his known trip with her to the doctor's office. The alleged father's close relationship with the mother, if she had no other close male relationships, is usually persuasive in proving paternity.

In other cases, the alleged father will have admitted his paternity by his words or conduct. For example, if the mother has a witness to show that, when she made her allegation of paternity, the scoundrel kept quiet, his silence suggesting an admission. In rare cases, physical resemblance between a child and the alleged father may be significant. Consider a situation in which the mother is a white, Caucasian female with fair skin, blonde hair, blue eyes and no distinguishing facial features, and the alleged father is a male, also white Caucasian, with fair skin, blonde hair, blue eyes and no distinguishing facial features. If the child resembles the alleged father, it would have no value, because the child could easily have inherited such characteristics from his mother. On the other hand, if the court finds that a child has a marked facial resemblance to the alleged father, and the mother is a full-blooded Indian, the court would be entitled to give weight to the child's looks.

Under the *Family Law Reform Act, 1978*, parents who are not living together and are not married may not make an agreement with respect to the custody of a child but may make an agreement that deals with the child's support. Besides support, the agreement can provide for the expenses of prenatal care, the expenses arising from the birth of the child, or any burial expenses of a child or the mother. If there is any suspicion as to the father's commitment to support the child, the agreement should definitely be incorporated into an order of the court, preferably on a lump sum rather than periodic payment basis. Going after a father for money is one of the less pleasant features of being a single mother. An actuary may be of assistance in determining the amount, but a lump sum payment of no less than $20,000.00 should be considered as an objective, realistic amount for supporting a child throughout his childhood. Keep in mind inflation, though, and special needs, and the old saying about "squeezing blood from a stone." It's a proverb you'll get used to hearing if you are going after the father for money in our courts.

Help in Raising a Child

Although child rearing is an expensive proposition, there are some tax benefits. If you are paying support for a child in accordance with a separation agreement or an order of the court, these payments are deductible from your taxable income. It is seldom realized that all expenses incurred — the bulk of which will be legal fees — in obtaining support for a child, or enforcement of an agreement or order, are also deductible from taxable income. If a mother spends $3,000 for a lawyer who is hired to enforce an order of the court, and collects $5,000 owing to her as payments not made by the father, that $3,000 can be deducted from her taxable income.

Children are dependants and qualify for deduction from taxable income for the person who has custody and is residing with them. In 1979, there is an exemption of $910 for a child sixteen years or older and $500 for a child under sixteen. However, when there is a separation a child can stand in place of a spouse and the custodial parent can receive a deduction of $2,650 for an "equivalent to married exemption". If one child is nine years, the other eighteen, a greater deduction can be made by letting the younger child stand in as the "equivalent to married exemption". It's allowed. Finally, deductions are permitted for each month a child is a full-time student at a post-secondary institution. $50 for each month at school is cumulatively added and the total is deducted from the custodial parent's taxable income.

Ontario has various pieces of legislation to assist families who are experiencing serious financial problems. The definitions of the various Acts are subject to change with every year, every budget constraint, and every election, but here is a summary of the relevant Statutes:

The Family Benefits Act: This provides for provincial long-term financial assistance to single and two parent families. A child cannot receive support in his own right under this Act, but graduated amounts of money are provided to the parent for each child so long as he is attending school, or is unable to attend by reason of a mental or physical disability, while remaining dependent on the parent.

The General Welfare Assistance Act: This Act directs the municipalities to provide temporary assistance to families in their jurisdiction. Under this Act, a child can be entitled to support in his own right between the ages of sixteen and eighteen if he can satisfy the city's welfare administrator that there exist "special circumstances" to justify his request. Note that any child should be entitled to emergency assistance for a period of two weeks even before the discretion of the administrator is invoked;

The Health Insurance Act: This Act enacts insurance schemes covering health services performed by a medical physician or practitioner, such as a chiropractor, or a podiatrist. Anyone under the age of twenty-one years, or mentally or physically disabled, is covered under his parent's plan. If that person is not dependent on the parents for support, he can apply for his own plan and if his income is low enough, he can also apply for full or partial premium assistance.

The Vocational Rehabilitations Services Act: This Act provides assistance to children who fall within the category of "disabled persons" and require rehabilitation or pre-vocational counselling and assistance. For example, a learning-disabled child who is under the age of sixteen years, and requires special educational services often unavailable at his own school, can seek assistance under this Act. Indeed, as a result of Ontario's general refusal to recognize the needs of children with learning disabilities, this Act has been heavily relied upon in the absence of appropriate educational resources.

The Day Nurseries Act: This Act enables the establishment of day nursery and private home day care as part of general day care assistance for Ontario families. The regulations under this Act provide for the accepted standards which must be met and the consumer should inform himself of the guidelines to insure adequate quality day care. The Act also calls for the provisions of financial assistance to those lower-income parents to qualify.

The Juvenile Delinquents Act: When a child is placed in the care of a Children's Aid Society or a group home residential setting under the Act, there are provisions in the Statute to seek support from the parents, or where the parents do not have sufficient funds, from the Municipality for any costs of special services to the child. (Recall our discussion in Chapter 2, where the Act was used to order a Municipality to pay $7800 to a private school for the costs of the child's attendance there, the child ordered to go to the school as part of the disposition of the court.)

As well as liability for direct monthly payments, the issue of support necessarily includes the question of whether the child is to remain in the family home. Often he will be forced to uproot himself, finding alternative and, very probably, less expensive accommodation with the custodial parent. Until recently, the law determining ownership and possession of the matrimonial home was rooted in the general rules of property law, with some discretion in the court to award possession temporarily to one spouse over the other, depending on all of the circumstances. The right to possession vested in one spouse overrode the right of the other spouse to sell or dispose of the home in any way.

The new *Family Law Reform Act, 1978* spells out the criteria to underlie this discretion, placing the child squarely in the middle, "if in the opinion of the court other provisions for shelter are not adequate in the circumstances, or it is in the best interests of the child to do so". One Ontario court viewed the matter thusly:

> Whether a wife was justified in leaving the respondent or not, she does have custody of the children and as of the 1st of September, she must find a place for herself and the children to live in . . . . The wife's difficulties far outweigh the inconvenience to the husband of moving at this time. Moreover, it is of considerable concern that the children be subjected to the minimum number of moves, and the minimum disturbances to the normal pattern of their lives.[18]

Apart from the issue of which children are entitled to support, there remains the question of *quantum*, or what amount the judge should order. Obviously amounts will vary, but one justice has defined the ideal sum as one "which would be adequate to care for, support and educate the children, dividing the sum in proportion to the respective income and resources of the parents, and directing the payment of the appropriate proportion by the parent not having physical custody."

As an alternative to court proceedings, the parties can enter into a private contract dealing with support and custody of the children. However, as in the case of all agreements concerning children, it can be set aside by the courts if it compromises the welfare of the child. In addition, any child support order or agreement can be varied by the courts if there is a material change in circumstances between the time the original order or agreement was made and the time of the application. For instance, if one of the parties remarries, and assumes added family responsibilities by becoming a father to the children of his new spouse, this may be considered a material change in circumstances legitimately reducing that person's ability to pay support for his biological children.

5

GETTING HEARD: REPRESENTATION

The Court: You cannot continue, Jeannie. Even though what you are saying your sister told you is true, in your opinion, we cannot accept this as evidence of the truth unless she is here in court to say it.

Jeannie: But Judge, I know my sister and one thing is true, you can trust her...

The Court: That may be true but the law requires...

Jeannie: (interrupting) You don't trust *me*. That's it isn't it?
—*From a court transcript.*[19]

If you have ever seen a child struggle to open a door *just* far enough to barely slip through, then you have some perspective on the power of children under Canadian law. It is less the closed door itself that threatens the child than his helpless inability to cause the door to open. Legal rights for children hinge upon their power to achieve identity and personal integrity in a state, which, when confronted with the child's demands for recognition, replies with charitable condescension. There is too much charity and not enough empathy, respect, or even tolerance for the child. Consequently, the cardinal rule for the child caught in a bind, be it a court room, a group home, a lock-up, a police station, or a principal's office, is to insure that he has with him someone as big and as powerful as his accusor. That is, the child, like any other person whose rights are threatened, needs, and is entitled to, a legal representative, "his gunslinger", to ensure a fair balancing of power.

Take, for example, the fifteen-year-old boy placed by the Children's Aid Society in a residential setting near Barrie,

Ontario. The child was found to be difficult to handle by the staff, and, as a result of his "acting out" was put in an isolated garage known to both staff and the children as "Birmingham Jail". This structure had a bare cement floor and was furnished with an army cot and a boxer's punching bag (presumably for the purpose of cooling off). The child would not accept this form of punishment and retaliated, as he saw it, by insisting that he eat his meals with the other children in the house, and that, in view of the November weather, he be allowed to sleep in his bedroom rather than in the non-heated "jail". His demands to be heard resulted in an angry confrontation; he kicked the kitchen table and damaged the house telephone. The agency staff called in the police, and on being charged with various minor offences, the boy was taken to the Barrie jail where he remained for some five days.

After being isolated in this adult jail, the child appeared in the Juvenile Court to find himself alone, pitted against both the placement staff and a representative of the Children's Aid Society. Reluctantly, he pleaded guilty to the offence of "committing a delinquency" under the *Juvenile Delinquents Act*; to wit, of wilfully damaging the telephone. A recommendation was presented to the court that he be sent to training school for an indefinite period of time. At no time was the child informed of his rights to be represented, to be granted an adjournment, to receive bail, to cross-examine witnesses, to give his own evidence, to receive any written report concerning sentence, or to appeal the decision of the court. Indeed, it seems that no one bothered to find out the child's story of what happened.

The case was passed on to another Juvenile Court, where at least the boy was given opportunity to speak, although still not represented by counsel. Here is a portion of the transcript from that trial:

> *The Court:* ...they are saying you are not being accountable for your own behaviour, answering for what you have done. Do you disagree with that?
>
> *The Child:* What does "accountable" mean?
>
> *The Court:* Account for what you do. You have the

responsibility to stand up and say "yes, I will accept the consequences for".

The Child: I can do that. I have done that, but they want me to sleep in a garage.

The Court: What do you feel hassled about? What is bothering you?

The Child: Well, they want me to sleep in a garage. I refuse to sleep in a garage with rats crawling around.

The Court: Well, why don't you say that?

The Child: I did. I told them that.[20]

If "accountable" was a hard word for the child, the convolutions of the "therapy" rationale presented at this trial by the staff of "Birmingham Jail" might as well have been in Chinese. The court soon allowed the child to obtain independent counsel, and later permitted the plea of guilty to be struck from the record.

The Canadian Bill of Rights

This child was entitled to legal counsel at a much earlier stage, certainly, because he was subject to a proceeding under the *Juvenile Delinquents Act.* Therefore, he was a defendant in a criminal proceeding and entitled to full citizen's rights. The Act is a Federal law, complying with the Canadian Bill of Rights, which provides (Section 2) that no law of Canada shall be construed or applied so as to:

(a) authorize or effect the arbitrary detention, imprisonment or exile of any person;

(b) impose or authorize the imposition of cruel and unusual treatment or punishment;

(c) deprive a person who has been arrested or detained

    (i) of the right to be informed promptly of the reason for his arrest or detention;

    (ii) of the right to retain and instruct counsel without delay, or

    (iii) a remedy by way of habeas corpus for the determination of the validity of his detention and his release if the detention is not lawful.

Section 2 of the Canadian Bill of Rights also provides that no law of Canada is to be construed or applied so as to:

(d) authorize a Court, Tribunal, Commission, Board or other authority to compel a person to give evidence if he is denied counsel, protection against self-incrimination and other constitutional safeguards;

(e) deprive a person of their right to a fair hearing in accordance with the principles of fundamental justice for the determination of his rights and obligations;

(f) deprive a person charged with a criminal offence of the right to be presumed innocent until proven guilty according to law in a fair and public hearing by an independent and impartial Tribunal, or of the right to reasonable bail without just cause.

Accordingly, unless children are not considered to be "persons", they should be assured the same protections under the Canadian Bill of Rights as any other accused person who is charged with an offence. Unfortunately, as we have seen, these protections are not always available to every child who is brought before the Juvenile Courts in Canada.

The right of a child to have counsel to assist him *without delay* is all the more important since, despite judicial guidelines, there is no clear law which requires a parent or equivalent to be present when a statement is taken from a child. Nevertheless, until the lawyer does arrive, the child should seek permission for a parent or a trusted friend to be present. If this request is made, many police authorities will allow that person to attend when the child is questioned. If the request is refused, the child has the right to remain silent and withhold information until he has had the opportunity to speak to a lawyer or to somebody else of his choice.

Types of Counsel

Choice of, and trust in, one's representative are integral to our advocacy system. Consider, however, the legislation which provides for probation officers to be assigned to Juvenile Courts. One of their duties includes the representation of the child before the court. Another of their duties is to furnish to the court all information about the child. To do both, at the same time, is not representation. Probation officers do not, in fact, represent children, and children should not accept a probation officer as a legitimate substitute for a lawyer. For one thing, information which the child provides to a probation officer is not privileged, as it is with a lawyer, and can be revealed to the judge in the probation officer's nebulous role of "assisting the court". This role might even compel the probation officer to reveal information which would lead to more charges being laid.

In some Juvenile Courts, the child will be exposed to a kind of representation through the assistance of a "duty counsel". Duty counsel is a lawyer available at the court house for people without their own counsel. In most juvenile cases, he will talk to the child for a few minutes before the hearing, and that will be the last the child hears of him. Although duty counsel may be of assistance in requesting an adjournment from the court for the purpose of obtaining a lawyer, the child should not accept this person as his representative in the actual hearing. There is too much at stake in a delinquency proceeding (not the least of which is the child's gaining a criminal record) to rely upon such a brief encounter with a stranger.

In practice, the child should not accept anyone as his lawyer unless that person can answer "yes" to the following three questions:

(1) Do you know about children's rights and children's law?

(2) Will you keep everything I tell you confidential unless you check with me first, and that includes talking to my parents?

(3) If I do not have money to pay you, will you help me to secure legal aid?

Having a lawyer who can answer these three questions affirmatively will provide the child with the kind of representation which is enjoyed by other members of our society.

Children can become entangled in legal processes through other than delinquency proceedings. Consider Jeannie, a thirteen-year-old child who, largely as a result of her parents' marital disputes, has sought refuge in the home of her Aunt Grace. Jeannie would like to live with her father, but mother opposes this idea, suggesting that Jeannie is uncontrollable and needs help. She calls upon the Children's Aid Society to assist her daughter. The child is brought to court by the Society, who alleges that as a result of the home situation, and its effect upon Jeannie's emotional state, she is a child "in need of protection" and should be placed in a residential setting for complete assessment. Aunt Grace is willing to provide a home for Jeannie, but is reluctant to become involved for fear of upsetting her sister-in-law. The Children's Aid Society has reservations about Aunt Grace's home in view of the antagonisms that exist between Jeannie's mother and her aunt, and the need for a complete assessment of the child in a neutral environment.

Representation and Child Welfare

If Jeannie, her mother and father, her aunt, and the Children's Aid Society are unable or unwilling to agree on an arrangement, and the State, through the Society, remains concerned about Jeannie's welfare, the court will be called upon to determine if the State is justified in intervening. Traditionally, the parties to a child welfare proceeding such as Jeannie's, would be the Children's Aid Society, or the Superintendent of Child Welfare, and each of the parents. Having the status of a "party" in a legal proceeding is significant, since certain rights thereby attach automatically. These rights are based on the principles of natural justice, including the right to be represented, the right to notice of hearing, the right to cross-examine and the right to appeal to another court.

Parents are parties to proceedings because they are the joint guardians of the child, and until ousted as the guardians, they are responsible for the child's welfare. In a child welfare hearing, the Children's Aid Society seeks to assume care of the child, and the parents' status as guardians is on the line. The Children's Aid Society or the Superintendent of Child Welfare may be a "party" because they represent the State in a role similar to that of a Crown Attorney in a criminal proceeding. Whereas the Crown represents the State in prosecuting those who have violated laws, the Children's Aid Society prosecutes those who have fallen short of providing the minimal standard of care which society expects in child rearing.

Unless a person is a party to a proceeding, the judge does not have to hear from him. Unlike a criminal proceeding, where the child is a defendant, and therefore a party, the allegedly neglected child has been entirely without party status in a child welfare hearing. The courts have generally looked upon the Children's Aid Society as representatives of the child, since they are incorporated for the purpose of protecting children's interests. However, in a case like Jeannie's, with a mother and father at war, and Aunt Grace not wanting to offend, and Jeannie herself labeled "uncontrollable", it's easy to see that the child's wishes could get lost in the turmoil. One Family Court Judge has stated that "if the *Child Welfare Act* considers the paramount interest of the children, then it is clear that children must be parties to the application; in fact, the most interested parties."[21] Other judges and legal experts agree, but as yet, in most provinces in Canada, the child does not have party status or the right of representation in cases involving his or her home, care, or maintenance.

It is true that in some provinces the court may hear any person on behalf of the child, but such testimony is allowed or requested at the discretion of the judge and many judges have concluded that if the Children's Aid Society and the parents are involved, there is no need for any further person to speak for the child. Even if a judge does recognize the need, such discretion is exercised at the time of the hearing, precluding a lawyer, for example, from working on behalf of his client out of court. By the time the matter proceeds to court, the conflict is usually heightened to such an extent that the court has no choice but to impose a decision upon the parties. If the court is to err, it will usually err on the side of safety for the child. In practical terms, this means that the child will be placed in the care of the Children's Aid Society as a child "in need of protection".

Recent and substantial amendments to Ontario's *Child Welfare Act*, proclaimed on June 15, 1979, provide the child with more rights in a protection proceeding that he has enjoyed in the past. Before delineating them, it should be remembered that these rights are on paper only, and a careful study of future cases will show whether there has been any real and substantive change. Implementation of rights is not automatic and, in this case, will be normally secured by those very adults who have spent years acting in the child's best interests without the assistance (or, to some, the interference) of a child's legal representative. In other words, unless a Children's Aid Society or the court requires that the child have access to counsel, legislating a right is of little use.

Section 20 of the amended Act breaks tradition in providing that a child may have legal representation at any stage in the proceeding involving the Children's Aid Society. This means that a lawyer who wishes to represent a child does not have to wait until the matter actually comes before the court. Once retained, he may take preventative measures immediately, including negotiation, mediation, or the finding of alternative community resources which could more suitably alleviate the problem.

If a child does not have legal representation, the court is empowered to appoint legal representation for the child, particularly where there is a difference in opinion among the views of the child, either parent, or the Children's Aid Society. The child, especially as an infant, may also need counsel if there are allegations of physical or mental abuse. An appointment of counsel will insure the judge of a more comprehensive presentation of information in light of the gray areas which always surround this type of neglect. Although the legal representative cannot take instructions from a young child or infant, he would be of assistance in bringing out information unavailable to or avoided by either the Children's Aid Society or the parents, who are necessarily polarized within the context of the adversarial judicial system.

Other considerations for the appointment of counsel might include the absence of any parent at the hearing concerning a child already in the care of the Children's Aid Society, or allegations that the child suffered abuse while protected by the Society. In one case, a thirteen-year-old child had been raped by her foster parent. The foster parent was subsequently charged in Criminal Court; the child was removed from the foster home and returned to her mother. Because the event heightened the already suspicious feelings of the mother and the child about Children's Aid and because the Society still wished to continue its involvement, a separate lawyer was appointed to represent the child. This appointment was a recognition by the court of the conflict among all three — Children's Aid, the child, and her family — and the use of the lawyer as mediator.

In some cases, if the child is not present in the court, because of his age or the undesirable effect of hearing allegations about his family, the court can appoint counsel so that the child's wishes and interests are made known. Also, if there is a difference in the viewpoints of the child and the Children's Aid Society or the parents, the court should appoint counsel on behalf of the child where the child appears without a legal representative. The effect of Section 20 of the amended Act is limited to proceedings involving the State, through its agent, the Children's Aid Society, in situations where the Society is alleging an intolerable state of care of the child. While the amended Act leaves unanswered the question of whether a child is a party to the proceeding, it does ensure the child the right to representation at any stage of the matter.

There are a number of further statutory changes which assist the position of a child within the context of the Child Welfare hearing:

(1) Under the amended Act, a child of twelve or more

years of age has the right, after the expiration of six months from the making of an order placing him under the supervision of the Children's Aid Society, or committing him into Society care as a ward of the Society or the Crown, to seek a review of his status. A child at the same stage has the right to seek access to any person he desires, and, as well, there can be no voluntary care agreement between the parents and the Society whereby the child lives outside of his home, without the consent of the child if he is twelve years of age or more, except in circumstances where the child is unable or incompetent to understand the agreement. In addition, if the child is capable of considering the agreement, he also has the right to seek review of any agreement.

(2) A child of ten or more years of age is entitled to be present at any hearings that are part of the child welfare proceedings, unless the court is satisfied that the effect of the hearing would be injurious to his emotional health, and conversely, a child under ten years of age is not to be present unless the court is of the opinion that his presence would not be injurious to his emotional health. A child of ten or more years of age is entitled to notice of all hearings, unless the court is satisfied that the effect of the hearing, or any part thereof, would be injurious to the emotional health of the child, in which case the court may direct that the child not be served with the notice.

(3) A child of ten years of age or more is entitled to receipt of any psychiatric assessment performed on either him or his parents, as ordered by the court, unless the court rules that to provide the child with a copy of the report would be detrimental to his interests. Finally, a child has a right through a "next friend" to appeal any decision made with respect to child welfare proceedings.

In Jeannie's situation, her own lawyer could ensure that all persons important to her own wishes are before the court: her aunt, her sister, her brother-in-law. Often, foster parents who have directly affected the child's life and who may know the child best are absent from the court; the lawyer should see that they come. If Jeannie's emotional welfare is in doubt, the lawyer might find independent and impartial sources to offer opinions. Most important, the lawyer must provide a child with some understanding of the court process, the power of the judge, the nature of the evidence, and the kind of evidence she can offer. He should offer support, reassurance, and a sense that the child has some measure of power and importance in the drama to come.

In Jeannie's case, she was hampered by something as apparently incidental as the changing of schools and the hassles about going to a school in an area in which her parents did not live. Providing Jeannie with the knowledge of how to get around this obstacle, and helping her in doing it, got rid of what was a major, almost obsessive concern of hers during the proceeding. For one thing, this problem was being manipulated by her mother and blown out of perspective as a means for convincing her daughter to stay at home. This kind of a problem rarely enters the court room, but it certainly affects the parties, and particularly the child, in their ability to participate as freely as possible, and with the least number of distractions from the central issue, the child's welfare.

The Lawyer's Responsibility

Admittedly, representing children means a different form of lawyering than representing an adult. Children do not know when, how, or why to call a lawyer when they are in need of one. However, that does not mean that they do not need legal help. The law has learned to accommodate and attempt to protect the unique needs of the master and servant, or the husband and the wife. Only when it begins to recognize the equally significant polarity of "big and small" — the adult and the child — will it then be able to successfully help the child.

One case in particular always comes to my mind in assessing our present helping system for children. A fifteen-year-old persisted in running away from the home in which the court had placed him. On becoming involved, I learned of the child's wishes to live with his grandfather in the interior of British Columbia. He had told this to the various social workers who had passed through his life over the preceding three years. (In fact, this desire to find and live with his grandfather was always the reason presented to his captors when he was picked up on one of his runs.) Unfortunately, information concerning even the existence of his grandfather had never been brought to the court's attention. As both mother and father were unable and unwilling to provide care for him, I set about to locate the child's grandfather, if only to inform my client of his whereabouts. After some two and a half months of investigation, I discovered that the man was dead. He had died three months before my client was born.

I was later told that my client had been told of his grandfather's death when he was younger. It seemed that in his pursuit for a sense of family, the fact of his grandfather's death had been repressed. The child had covered it up by clinging to the mystery of his grandfather, allegedly alive but missing — something like the child himself. This fifteen-year-old needed to be confronted with the fact of his grandfather's death so that living with him could be ruled out in his mind as a viable alternative. Fantasy dissolution is certainly familiar to the corporate lawyer who convinces his client that an entirely tax-free shelter does not exist. It is also a necessity to the matrimonial lawyer whose client, the non-custodial father, cries "destitution" in the face of child support because his assets are "tied-up". Can it be any less important a tool to the lawyer who represents children?

In Ontario, as in some of the other provinces, there exists a representative of the Provincial government known as the Official Guardian. Traditionally, the Official Guardian, who must be a lawyer of a minimum ten years experience, has been appointed to act as the child's "protector" in property matters. For example, if a child has a beneficial interest in an estate pursuant to a will, and the other beneficiaries wish to have the assets distributed, the Official Guardian is obliged to make representations with respect to the child's "best interests". However, in the recent past, this government agency has expanded its role to include representation in custody and child welfare proceedings. Ontario's Official Guardian approaches his role, whether it be a case of protecting a child's property or his emotional welfare, as being a spokesman for a child's best interests.

In a recent policy statement, the Office argues that the solicitor/client privilege, the rule of confidentiality between a lawyer and his client, should not apply when representing a child. Furthermore, while the wishes of a child may be articulated to the court when they coincide with the child's interest, counsel should remain silent when presenting the child's wishes in conflict with the child's interests. So much for representation. Few adults would retain a lawyer who spoke solely in their best interests rather than *for* them. Lawyers advise their clients as best they can, clarifying their legal position, possible alternatives and resulting implications, and giving the client a considered recommendation.

A thirteen-year-old on the run, a fifteen-year-old girl on the street refusing to go home, a nine-year-old afraid to go home for fear of being hit, an eleven-year-old learning-disabled child acting out in his classroom for want of adequate instruction can all be assisted by the lawyer acting as their *lawyer*, as opposed to their judge. Too many people already assess, worry about and invariably censor the child's desires in the name of his best interests. It shouldn't be daring to suggest that there be at least one adult participant working on the premise of the child's wishes, as opposed to the child's "best interests".

After a presentation of mine to the Canadian Bar Association, some skeptical representatives of the Official Guardian's Office posed a test-case, in which a thirteen-year-old girl had been sexually abused by her father, but wanted to continue living with him. Would I go so far as to advocate her position to the court? My questioner was of the opinion that the child was too young or too naive to give proper instructions, and it was obviously not in the best interests of the child to reside with her father.

My answer was that I would certainly represent her wishes and articulate her viewpoint to the best of my ability, including her desire to live with her father. That is my role as her lawyer. To listen to the child's desires to live with her father, and to represent her implicitly, acting upon her desires as the premise of any services, is not to condone sexual abuse. Indeed incestuous conduct is so complex a matter that any real assistance must incorporate all viewpoints and feelings, including those of a victim child. There is a great deal which a lawyer can do for a child as a client in this and other situations, while leaving the decision of "best interests" in the hands of the judge, where it belongs.

Children in The Court Room

With conflicting opinions clouding the entire field of children's law and children's counsel, it is not surprising that the child in the court room finds an *Alice in Wonderland* world of apparently arbitrary rules and taboos.

> "Have some wine", the March Hare said in an encouraging tone.
> Alice looked all around the table, but there was nothing on it but tea.
> "I don't see any wine", she remarked.
> "There isn't any", said the March Hare.
> "Then it wasn't very civil of you to offer it", said Alice.
> "It wasn't very civil of you to sit down when you weren't invited", said the March Hare.

A complex of evidentiary rules has evolved in our system of common law which serves to eliminate testimony in the court room likely to be unreliable and/or irrelevant. However, the rules are often obscure and confusing, especially to the child who has no representative to act as interpreter. Perhaps the most relevant rule for the lawyer representing the child, and therefore sensitive to the child's viewpoint, is that a person must swear, or affirm, under oath to tell the truth. If the person cannot understand the nature of swearing the oath, his testimony becomes "unsworn evidence" and therefore less credible. It is, in fact, evidence given without an assertion by the witness that it is the truth. In the case of a child as witness, the court is expected to conduct an inquiry to disclose the child's attitude towards telling the truth and his understanding of the meaning of the oath.

It is not necessary for the judge to conduct a spiritual inquisition of the child, nor is it necessary for the child to know the hellfire and brimstone consequences of not telling the truth. It is usually sufficient for the child to indicate that it is important to tell the truth and that it is wrong not to tell the truth.

The court must conduct this inquiry with any child of "tender years", which, as a rule of thumb, is under the age of fourteen. If the child understands the oath, he will be sworn and his evidence will theoretically be treated like that of any witness. However, there is a rule of practice directing trial judges to warn juries not to convict on the uncorroborated evidence of a child, and to weigh the evidence, even where sworn, with extreme caution. (Uncorroborated evidence is testimony by one person which has not been substantiated or confirmed by any other person or by any other means).

Where the child does not understand the nature of the oath, the judge must conduct a further inquiry to determine whether the child is possessed of sufficient intelligence to justify the admission of his evidence, and whether the child understands the duty of speaking the truth. If these conditions are satisfied, unsworn testimony can be heard, although the final decision cannot be based on it alone, but must be supported by corroboration. Consider this inquiry which was held to be satisfactory for a child giving sworn evidence:

Q. How old are you?

A. Fourteen.

Q. What grade are you in?

A. Eight.

Q. Have you ever given evidence in court before?

A. Well, at the preliminary trial.
Q. Preliminary hearing?
A. Yes.
Q. Do you know what it is to take an oath?
A. Yes.
Q. You do, what is it?
A. Well, it is to tell the truth.
Q. Fine.
A. Not to lie. It is no good. You may as well not say anything at all.
The Court: Fine, I will accept that.

Whether or not the child is competent as a witness, the courts do invoke an apparently discretionary power to prohibit the child from being called as a witness. The courts use the power of their *parens patriae* (the state as parents) jurisdiction to *supervise* the child amidst the adversarial process. One judgment of the Supreme Court gives us a comprehensive illustration:

> There was some matter of evidence to which I now wish to make special reference...Counsel stated he had instructions to call as a witness, Michael, eleven, now living with his father. I said that I cannot prevent any witness being called, but I strongly disapproved of the involvement of children in the family disputes of their parents, unless it were impossible to prove the necessary facts in any other way. Here it seemed to me that the evidence already adduced for the father was comprehensive, clear and full on the issues involved. The witness could be called, but I advised against it. I said that, if it were necessary in my judgment, I would see the children later...
>
> The children were not called. I do not consider this to be a case in which I need to interview the children. In proceedings such as these where the welfare of the children and the future of the family is in the care of the court, it seems not only reasonable but desirable and necessary that the

judge should have some discretion to prevent the dispute between the parents becoming, as it might here, a dispute on oath between children as to the parent's merits and conduct. In some cases that may be necessary. It goes against the grain of family life and uses the court to set brother against brother. It should not be done where an impartial judge, able to be fully informed otherwise, does not consider it necessary.[22]

As the court indicates, one option in lieu of the child as a witness is to interview him privately. It is not improper for a trial judge sitting in a custody dispute to interview a child in his chambers, upon application by counsel on his behalf, or on behalf of either parent. Where the judge seeks a child, the judge should not allow the child's comments to be the sole basis for his judgment. Furthermore, courts have held that these discussions are to be fully disclosed to the parties so that they might have an opportunity of assessing and replying to the child's statements.

In addition to matrimonial cases, the desirability of a child as a witness was considered during a criminal proceeding in which the child's foster father was alleged to have killed his mother in the presence of the child. Although defence counsel wanted the child to testify, the Children's Aid Society, who had custody of the child, argued that the very presence of the child in the court room in such a hearing rendered him a "child in need of protection". The Family Court found that the child's presence did not warrant the court's finding of "protection", but that in any event, a finding of "protection" would not eliminate the child from the judicial process. Although the child may be called as a witness in almost all proceedings, there are rules restricting his presence in various forums:

(1) *The Juvenile Delinquents Act* provides that no child other than an infant in arms, shall be permitted to be present in any court during the trial of any person charged with an offence or during any proceeding

preliminary to the actual trial. And, if so present, the
child is to be removed unless he is the person charged
with the offence or unless his presence is required as a
witness or otherwise for the purpose of justice.

(2) *Ontario's Child Welfare Act, 1978* provides that any
child under the age of ten years, and who is the subject
of a proceeding concerning his welfare shall not be
present at a hearing unless the court is satisfied that
the hearing or any part thereof hearing would be
understandable to the child and would not be
injurious to his mental health. Conversely, the Act
provides that a child of ten or more years is entitled to
be present at a hearing or any part thereof unless the
court decides that the effect of the hearing or any part
would be injurious to the mental health of the child.

(3) In civil proceedings, it appears that the Supreme
Court of Ontario might have jurisdiction to exclude a
child on the basis of its inherent jurisdiction to protect
the interests of the children. Such power would likely
be exercised where the evidence, if heard by the child,
would be injurious to his emotional welfare.

Where a child is called as a witness, but refuses to come or
give evidence, he is subject to a citation of the court for con-
tempt like any other person, and the citation would also extend
to any adult who prevents the child from attending.

Helping and Testifying: The Social Worker

Related to the issue of the child as a witness and the ability of
the lawyer to represent the child is the question of the professional as a witness. Here, too, the question of the desirability of
the professional (as a witness) is raised. On the one hand, the
therapist, or the social worker, offers to the court an explanation of the dynamics of the child and the family based on his
perception of the client's internal or external realities. On the
other hand, the lawyer as interrogator phrases his questions in
accordance with the rigid rules of evidence, which ruthlessly

seeks "facts", eliminating "impressions" and broad generalizations.

Perhaps more frustrating than the evidentiary contradictions are those associated with the issue of confidentiality. Although most professional associations support the principles of confidentiality as part of their ethics, once the matter is before the court, other considerations emerge:

> That the public policy involved in this action, namely the welfare and future of the infant child, dominates over any of the public policies that have been heard before me in argument and is, in any event, the public policy which is my duty to serve in considering the issue in this case.[23]

This judicial statement was made during a case in which a witness refused to testify because, as a representative of the John Howard Society, he felt disclosure of information obtained from his client would be contrary to public policy as being detrimental to the trust relationship between the discharged prisoner and the agency. In contrast, the court, in another case, has held that statements made by divorcing spouses in the process of conciliation counselling should be privileged communication and not compellable in court. The judge gave priority to the aspect of confidentiality, thereby promoting counselling and the basis upon which parties enter into it. The issue continues in the courts.

Various lawyers and professional counsellors will clarify the role of the counsellor by referring to the counselling as "open" in which case the rules of confidentiality do not apply and the mediating counsellor can be called to court to report on all discussions by either party. "Closed" counselling suggests that confidentiality prevails, that all that is said within the counselling will not be disclosed to the court. The mediating counsellor prepares his report to the court, and it is only with respect to that report that either party may cross-examine.

Whatever route is agreed upon by the parties, the approach to be taken by most courts would probably be the compelling of testimony with respect to all information if such information is necessary to make an informed decision concerning the child's interest, excepting discussions between spouses for the purpose of reconciliation pursuant to proceedings under the *Divorce Act*, and any discussions between the lawyer and his or her client. As we noted in Chapter 2 there is no discretion or any question of "professional ethical considerations" when child protection is in issue. All professionals, save and except the lawyer in a solicitor and client relationship, must report information of the abandonment, desertion or need of protection of any child, failure of which can result in a fine of up to $1,000. Section 49(2) of the *Child Welfare Act* immunizes the informant from any action against him or her for so reporting unless the reporting was done maliciously or without reasonable grounds to suspect that the information is true. Furthermore, judicial decisions in England have held that the Children's Aid Society should not be compelled to disclose the identity of that person who reports to them an incident of abandonment, desertion or neglect.

Representation in Custody and Divorce

Having considered the question of representation in child protection and delinquency proceedings, and the various rules of evidence, there remain several other forums affecting the child's interest, one of which is custody and access disputes between spouses. Although the Judge makes an order as to custody and access, there is nothing to ensure the child's representation in his own right. If the question arises in a divorce proceeding, the *Divorce Act* (Canada) applies, and the court has the power to appoint the Official Guardian, or any other lawyer, to act as *guardian ad litem* to the child — that is, guardian for the purpose of dealing with the issue before the court. Ontario's *Family Law Reform Act, 1978* allows the Provincial Court (Family Division) where the issue of custody and access arises independent of a divorce proceeding, to give such directions for the representation of a child as it deems appropriate if satisfied that the interests of the child are involved in a proceeding.

No similar provision exists in the rules with respect to proceedings under the *Family Law Reform Act, 1978* in the County or Supreme Courts, but those courts do have the power to appoint the Official Guardian, or any solicitor, as *guardian ad litem* to that child. Moreover, the court is entitled on its own application, or upon application by any of the parties to the proceeding, to hold a pre-trial conference, at which time various issues, including that of representation for the child can be considered.

In allowing the judge, rather than the parties, to appoint the child's representative, the possibility of either parent manipulating the choice to his or her advantage is eliminated. However, once appointed, representation should include those duties as outlined in this chapter, the foremost function of the lawyer which is to present the client's viewpoint to the best of his ability.

And yes, children can hire their own lawyer. It takes a certain kind of lawyer to want to represent a child, mind you. It depends upon the age of the child, for it is difficult for even the most sincere, dedicated lawyer to argue his ability to represent a five-year-old without the consent of the child's guardian, or failing that, the approval of the court. Legislation tends to create arbitrary assignment of ages to aspects of childhood since it deals with rules for the general population. However, each case of representing a client is unique, and no general rule can effectively operate as to when a child has the ability to benefit from an independent spokesman. As a signal for myself, I have found that any child who independently contacts me or causes his social worker or parent so many problems that he is referred to me, can usually benefit from a lawyer. Children "on the street", those fugitives within our urban collectives, are as able to benefit from a lawyer as any adult I have represented. The only distinction, in many ways, concerns their ability to pay. The fourteen-year-old street girl could easily appear to be a spousal alimony case until her opening words at a first interview reveal her problem as one of truancy.

Legal Aid

Children usually don't have money and there are only so many pop bottles that any person can collect. Children can obtain legal aid, just as any other person who doesn't have enough money to afford a lawyer. Legal Aid officials may request information showing that the child cannot rely on his parents for the cost of legal services, either because of a parent/child conflict, or because the child lives outside the home, independent of his parents, or because the parents cannot afford it. In Ontario, matters may become complicated since, apparently, the Legal Aid Directors are advising children that the Official Guardian can represent them, and where alternative government resources exist for representation, the Director is entitled by the Legal Aid Regulations to refuse a certificate. In a way, a monopoly of sorts is beginning to take shape in the Official Guardian's Office, which will, no doubt, offer the flexibility of any monopoly, along with the added force of institutional bureaucracy and representation.

If this policy continues without revision, the right of a fifteen-year-old to choose his or her own lawyer will be denied, because in practice, the lawyer chosen will not be able to be guaranteed payment unless approved by the overriding supervisor, the Official Guardian. Lawyers, like doctors, make different diagnoses of the same problem and have different ways of dealing with the same problem, usually to the benefit of the client or the patient. With the advent of the Official Guardian's office into the representation of children outside the arena of property concerns, that benefit appears to be unavailable to the child.

Next, we'll look at the obstacles facing anyone who, in his or her own right, wants to help a child in our society, despite the institutional red-tape, the patronizing officials, the runarounds and the put-downs. It's an up-hill battle, but it's worth it, and it's needed. Institutionalizing help for children only institutionalizes the problems, and institutionalizing problems is our most trustworthy method of avoiding problems altogether. Worse still, all our organizations and tangled rules only make it harder for the community to confront the problems of the child and the child's family. Creating more and varied guardians, not to mention official ones, takes us farther away from helping, not closer.

6

HELPING CHILDREN: LIMITATIONS AND LIABILITIES

Director, Children's Aid Society: I wonder if I might, and I know this is a court of law, and there are rules by...

The Court: Do you want to say something now?

Director: Yes, and you might find it disrespectful and you might feel...

The Court: If it is, I will let you know.

Director: ...it is of a conceited nature, but I do not intend it to be that, but I am a behavioral scientist and I find here that we have such a mixture of the legal process and the communicative therapies and modes of observation...I frankly think it isn't quite fair, if you don't mind my saying so.

The Court: I do.[24]

Helping children within the legal process means calling on the resources of many disciplines. Children on the street need all types of advice on birth control, employment, health care, and finances, but unfortunately children are often confused by the jargon and disagreements within the professions which compound the kids' already profound suspicion of authority. Moreover, the helping professional is often faced with the threat of his own legal liability should he help a child without the proper sanctions; there are legal rules which set down the limits for helping others, and they can hamstring the doctor or counsellor who wishes to treat or to help a child.

Under our law, application of force against another person without lawful consent or justification amounts to assault or battery, regardless of the degree or force, or whether it is intended or is able to do any real harm to the person. This assault, from a medical perspective, can range from surgical treatment to the prescription of a birth control pill. Application of force incurs no liability for the doctor where it is lawful; that is, where there is either justification for the touching or consent by the person touched.

Treatment based on the consent of the child, however, is suspect, since the law questions a child's capacity to consent. Traditionally, the age of consent is also the age of majority (which is eighteen in the Province of Ontario) and until this age, the medical profession usually seeks parental consent except in an emergency situation. Where a doctor acts unreasonably in providing medical advice to a child without the consent of the parents, he opens the door to a suit based on negligence. If a negligence suit is contemplated, then, unlike a suit based on assault and battery, there must be injuries for there to be any recovery of any damages.

Ontario's *Public Hospitals Act* provides an exception to this age of majority rule by allowing a surgical operation to be performed on a patient, or an out-patient, with consent in writing signed by a person sixteen years of age or over. The definition of "patient" and "out-patient" restricts its application to persons received in a hospital for examination or treatment, and "hospital" is restricted to those institutions so named and approved by the Act. Because of the selective application, the anomaly arises wherein a female may consent to an abortion, as a surgical operation in public hospital, but she may not be old enough to get necessary consent to receive contraceptive help through the insertion, for example, of an intra-uterine device in a doctor's office or a public health unit.

The Liberated Kid: Health, Sex and Money

Recently, there has emerged the legal concept of the "emancipated or mature minor", an individual generally between the ages of sixteen and eighteen years. If, in the assessment of a Judge, the individual is capable of understanding the consequences and nature of specific treatment, regardless of chronological age, consent would be valid. To come to the conclusion that the child is so capable, the court has to consider the maturity of the child, the child's dependence upon his guardians, the child's residence outside the home or outside of parental influence, and the complexity of the treatment.

What about a child of seventeen who is living away from home and supporting herself, her parents assuming little, if any, responsibility for her welfare? Various court decisions have supported the proposition that the doctor providing treatment to this child would not need her guardian's consent, so long as the treatment was found to be for the child's benefit. Note that where a person under the age of eighteen demands emergency treatment, consent is not the issue, since traditional law, as well as the Ontario *Public Hospitals Act* permits the doctor to act immediately.

Consider further the case of a fifteen-year-old girl who attends a public health clinic, requesting the insertion of an intra-uterine device. Despite the seeming maturity of the girl and her ability to comprehend the nature of the treatment, one must still consider whether or not the treatment is beneficial to the child. If not, then the doctor is rendering himself liable to an assault charge, either criminally or civilly. It is also possible that the doctor might be charged with "contributing to juvenile delinquency", since delinquency can include "...sexual immorality or any similar form of vice...". Under Section 33 of the *Juvenile Delinquents Act* a person may be charged with contributing to juvenile delinquency if his action allows the child to continue the delinquency. For a parent to dispute the benefit of birth-control treatment for his child, he must also allege that the prescription of birth-control medication contributes to the child's delinquency, if not directly, than indirectly, by permitting the child to continue behaving in a "sexually immoral manner". Admittedly, the Crown would have a difficult task asserting that the prescription of birth control was not done primarily to protect the child's health, but to contribute *knowingly* to, and to encourage, sexual immorality.

To validate this position, a positive connection between the prescription of contraceptives and the child's sexual immorality would have to be demonstrated, a connection not supported by most studies. In fact, the various Acts presently provide that all forms of contraceptives may be sold without any criminal sanction and that all forms of contraceptives may be advertised to the general public, except for intra-uterine devices. That is, it is not against public policy for any person, including the doctors, to advertise, sell or presumably counsel the use of contraceptive devices to anyone in general, or to children specifically. In one Australian case, the court held that the selling of contraceptives did not amount to contributing to the child's juvenile delinquency. The court concluded that the actual living conditions of the child would have to be examined in order to determine whether, in the first place, the child was lapsing, or was likely to lapse, into a career of vice, and secondly, whether the defendant, who in this case sold the contraceptives, caused, or could be said to have contributed to, the unsatisfactory living conditions of the child.

Doctors can escape legal repercussions in the courts on the consent issue only to find themselves subject to discipline from the governing bodies. In one British Columbia case, a doctor was found guilty by his medical association of "infamous or unprofessional conduct" in inserting a birth control device in a fifteen-year-old female patient without parental consent. On appeal to the courts, the doctor argued that the ethical rule of doctor/patient confidentiality should extend to the child's parents. The judge responded by noting that in some circumstances, the doctor's contentions might be true, but the conduct of a physician in any particular situation is a matter to be decided by his own professional governing board, as was done in the case against him, and the appeal was dismissed.

Therapy and Special Counsel

Counselling is a much less well-regulated and precise profession than medicine. Provincial legislation governs the practice of medicine and boards regulate the licensing of medical practitioners, but there are many types of professionals in the field of child care — psychologists, social workers and child-care workers — on whom the law does not appear to impose any rules or regulations. Where, however, counselling involves the application of force, such as physical restraint or holding, common sense suggests that the mature child or parent fully understand the nature and consequences of the treatment.

In one case, a mother and father approved the placement of their child in a group home. They signed the usual blanket consent forms providing the group-home staff with general authority to have care and control of the child. The parents had no idea, and understandably so, that punishment at the group home involved washing walls, being confined to one's room for a whole day, or being held down on the floor with a staff member sitting on top — allegedly provoking the child to "ventilate" his feelings. No consent form can provide immunity from a civil suit based on negligence; however, a consent form that is specific and gives the parent and the child a clear picture of the techniques for helping may prevent a later dispute.

In most cases, counselling services will expose the helping professional to a different kind of liability than that outlined above. If treatment by a counsellor is confined to "counselling" or "advising", then children may be so treated without parental consent, subject to the following guidelines:

Harbouring: A child of fourteen may not be kept in a hostel or a group home against the wishes of the parents. A counsellor may not interfere with the parent's right to physical custody, as he may otherwise be liable to a charge of harbouring under Section 250 of the Criminal Code. It would seem that there has to be proof that the counsellor knew the child's age to sustain a conviction.

Abduction: A counsellor may not provide accommodation or perform any action in which he "takes or causes to be taken" a female child under the age of sixteen out of the possession of and against the will of her parent or guardian: Section 249 of the Criminal Code. Unlike the first guideline with respect to children under the age of fourteen, it is not a defence to the counsellor that he believed the female child to be over the age of sixteen years, or even that the child came of her own will or suggestion. Note, however, that in respect of these two instances, there is no strict liability upon a counsellor to notify a parent when the child comes to him for assistance. Both Sections require a finding that the third party *intended* to deprive the parent of possession of the child. This requirement is independent of whether or not the child came of her own will. For example, a child, effectively "living on the street", may be sheltered by a third party in circumstances in which there is no intention to *deprive* the parent of possession, mostly because either parent is not in the picture.

Interference: A counsellor may not interfere with a "child" under the age of twenty-one years where the child has been placed in a home, a foster home, school or institution by the Juvenile Court. Interferences include any inducement or attempt to induce a child to leave such a place, or simply the action of knowingly harbouring or concealing such a child without notice to the Juvenile Court, the home or institution where the child has left, or the police. This Section, therefore, requires the counsellor to notify the appropriate authorities.

Ontario's *Child Welfare Act* makes it an offence if someone interferes with children who have been lawfully placed pursuant to the provisions of that Act. No one can "induce or attempt to induce a child to leave the care of an organization where the child has been lawfully placed, nor can a person detain or harbour a child who is lawfully in the care of a person or persons, without the consent in writing of the Children's Aid Society having the care, custody or supervision of the child". For the offence to crystallize, it is necessary that the authorities first require the person to deliver up the child. It is also an offence in Ontario to visit, write to, telephone, communicate with, or otherwise interfere with a child who is in the lawful care of a Children's Aid Society, or with the foster parent who has lawful care or custody of the child, unless there is an order providing for access under the *Child Welfare Act*, or unless consent is obtained from the Children's Aid Society.

False imprisonment: There is nothing in the role of the professional counsellor, barring Statutory provision, that absolves the counsellor of possible charges of kidnapping or false imprisonment. Accordingly, it is incumbent upon the counsellor to assure himself that the child has come of his own free will to seek assistance.

Contributing to juvenile delinquency: In view of the offence of "contributing to juvenile delinquency", a counsellor should insure that he does not, however indirectly, assist or abet the commission of any act known to be an offence although passive acquiescence is properly not sufficient. Furthermore, mere reception of information about an offence, or possible offence, committed by a child will not amount to contributing to juvenile delinquency. This Section, if read in line with judicial decisions, does not seem to require a person to be an informer or to report to the police any suspicions he may have concerning an offence.

Guardians and Consent

If the child has been made a "ward" under the *Child Welfare Act* or the *Training Schools Act*, guardianship is transferred from the parents to the state agency. Consequently, consent is no longer necessary from the parents of the child, but rather from the legal guardian, who, in the case of the *Child Welfare Act*, would be the local Children's Aid Society, and in the case of the *Training Schools Act*, would be the superintendent of the training school in which the child has been placed. In contrast, under Canada's *Juvenile Delinquents Act*, a child may be committed to the "care and custody of a probation officer or of any other suitable person" or be placed in a "suitable family home as a foster home", both of which are not sufficient to imbue that person or the placement agency with the power to provide or consent to treatment for the child. For example, if a child commits an offence, and the court determines that it is in the child's best interest to be placed in a group home in the care and custody of its director, the staff has no authority to provide or consent to treatment for the child without the express consent of the child's guardian, which, in this case would continue to be the parents. In order for guardianship to be transferred, there must be a specific order of the court.

Where parents are separated and one parent has custody by way of a separation agreement, that parent may place a child in the care of a residential facility. Ideally, the residential agency should seek consent not only from the parent who has custody, but also from the non-custodial parent, since, barring a court order, the non-custodial parent still possesses guardianship powers. Practically, such consent is not always possible, nor is it sought by the agency because the law is somewhat unclear. There is the alternative opinion that the custodial arrangements pursuant to a separation agreement are sufficient for an agency to provide treatment to the child with the consent of the custodial parent only.

The alternative opinions do not help the child. In one case, a mother, awarded custody by a separation agreement, enrolled her child in a summer camp without the father's knowledge. When the father found out, he protested a violation of his visiting rights. The mother had adopted the name of her common-law spouse for herself and her children, and the camp director, unaware of the facts, was refusing the father admission to the camp. Here the situation got very ugly. The father followed one of the camp buses, overtook it, and removed his child by force — a traumatic experience, certainly, for the child, the driver, and the twenty or so other children on the bus.

Until the law clears up the matter completely, accepting a signature from a parent for a child's admission into any program should only be done after a full inquiry of any other parent. The consent form should include an acknowledgment by the signing parent with respect to any other parent's whereabouts, and his or her knowledge of the intended admission of the child. Some agencies will allow a child between the ages of sixteen and eighteen to sign admission and consent forms for themselves on the basis that the child is an "emancipated minor" and need not bother to obtain consent from the legal guardian. This practice is highly suspect, since, as a general rule, the onus may be extremely heavy upon the agency in showing that the child was capable of appreciating the consequences and nature of the treatment.

Institutions apply various techniques in their care of children, and details about any special kind of care should be included in the consent form, clearly forewarning the guardian. Unless these techniques are listed in the specific consent, problems as discussed earlier could result. Some of the techniques I have encountered include:

Time out: This is a behavioral conditioning approach when a child is removed from other children and confined for a specific period of time because the child has acted inappropriately. The child is to learn through a number of these "ostracizing" experiences that, for example, spitting at another child is wrong. It's something like, "Go to your room until you learn how to behave," although all sorts of charts and monitoring devices are used to "temper frequency of inappropriate behaviour," according to the jargon.

Segregation: This involves removal of a child from the mainstream of a program to a "place of safety", such as an isolation room with a particular staff member who is assigned full-time to the child and who remains in contact with the child, utilizing direct confrontation. This approach was used with one fifteen-year-old girl I represented. Every time the child tried to run away, which reached nineteen times in 15 days, she was assigned to a certain male staff member. The female staff felt they could not handle her "aggression". It seemed that the child had developed a crush on her therapist amidst the "controlled confrontation", and running away guaranteed the return of her beloved.

Holding: As the name suggests, this is a physical restraining of a child by one or more staff members to help him express negative emotions safely, or to protect the child or others from his destructive impulses. Trained staff will know how to hold a child constructively — that is, in a way which protects the child while comforting him or her. Being held in order to protect oneself and to protect one from others need not be a violent, explosive situation, although agencies who simply sit on children in order to control them should expect some hostile reaction.

Physical restraint: This technique offers restraint by such mechanical means as a strait-jacket. It is a technique used in crisis situations when other means are not feasible, protecting the child from self-mutilation or protecting others from his aggressive behaviour. "Careful" is the word when applying this technique. When children are angry and cannot release it because of mechanical restraints, they often turn that anger inward and a therapist can have, along with a guilty conscience, a self-mutilation on his hands, even a suicide.

Medication: This generally refers to the use of injections rather than oral medication to calm an anxious or depressed youngster, or to control "acting out" in a crisis situation. The administration of medication by injection can only be done by a duly qualified physician or by a registered nurse. As well, medication must be prescribed according to the regulations of the *Health Disciplines Act*: Regulation 579/75.

In view of the disparity in therapeutic techniques, it is advisable that all parties, including the child, prior to placement, agree to, or at least be made aware of, these items:

(1) The techniques will be used only when less-restraining methods have failed;

(2) The techniques will never be used simply to obtain compliance with adult requests:

(3) The techniques will never be used for the purpose of punishment; and

(4) Management of drug medication assures no addiction will result.

If a child is in the custody of the Children's Aid Society or training school, consent to the use of these treatment techniques is still necessary and must be obtained from either the local director or the superintendent of the training school.

Confidentiality in Treatment

Some mention should be made of the question of confidentiality when children are involved with the various professionals outside the court room. *The Mental Hospitals Act*, dealing with the administration of psychiatric institutions, states that a disclosure of patients records may be made only upon order of the court, or if requested by the Director of the Psychiatric Hospitals Branch. Pursuant to Section 13 of Ontario Regulation 271, a regulation under the *Children's Mental Health Centre Act*, the Director of a children's Mental Health Services has the *sole* authority to examine all case files. This legislation prevents the mental health centres from revealing a patient's records unless required by a court order.

Within the various helping professions, there are no guidelines specifically designed to insure confidentiality. However, this is an issue which normally is dealt with by professional bodies and included in their code of ethics. Generally speaking, there must be informed consent for the release of any information on a client and whether a child can give a release will depend on factors similar to those related to his ability to consent to treatment. If he cannot give the appropriate release, then it would be obtained from his legal guardian. The release should be specific as to the information to be divulged, to whom it is to be released, and the extent to which the information is to be used. For example, the release should always indicate if the information pertaining to the child is to be used for the purpose of a film, a video-tape, a professional publication or experimental data.

One child had apparently attempted suicide, according to the records of a former mental health facility. The records did not indicate, as evidence at a later court hearing showed, that there was strongly divided opinion about her intent. Was she really trying to kill herself? The child had scratched her wrists until they bled, and this piece of information had travelled with her, making a new placement incredibly difficult. She had not, in fact, *slashed* her wrists, nor was there hard evidence that she was contemplating self-destruction. At any rate, neither the child nor her parents had ever consented to the release of such information, since the child was a ward of the Children's Aid Society, and that agency, as the child's legal guardian, had provided a general blanket consent form.

If a child is capable of signing these forms, then he is entitled to the same confidentiality extended to any other patient, even as against his parents. This situation often occurs when a child attends a clinic for drug-related medical assistance, or for birth control medication and, in either case, requests that a doctor not inform his parents. If a doctor finds the child is capable of signing the appropriate consent for treatment, then confidentiality should attach thereto.

One exception to the principle of confidentiality involves the treatment for venereal disease. The *Venereal Diseases Preventions Act* directs that all notices, directions or orders that are required or authorized by the Act for the purpose of treating and containing venereal disease shall be given to the mother or father, or to the person having custody of the child under the age of sixteen years who is infected or believed to be infected with a venereal disease. According to this Act, it is also the duty of the parent or other person who has custody, to see that the child complies in every respect with whatever order, notice or direction is given.

Who Pays The Bills?

One of the major obstacles to consulting professional people is that requirement of fees for services, and monetary power is not a child's strong suit. However, this usually is not a factor when the child or family is involved with the Children's Aid Society where funding is provided by the State. What about confidentiality when a parental health insurance plan or a government agency is footing the bill? Here, a doctor has the option to ensure confidentiality by indicating to the insurance plan that the account is to be "non-audited". In other words, the services provided to the child by the doctor listed in his account will not be checked with the insured parent, thus avoiding an indirect breach of confidentiality. Where children are placed in the care of a Children's Aid Society, or a training school, problems with respect to the Ontario Health Insurance Plan will be worked out with the Agency. (Where children are placed with a private agency, such as Browndale or Youthdale, the agency will usually require information from the guardians as to their Ontario Health Insurance Plan number so that they can obtain coverage for the child on that policy, if necessary.)

A lawyer's fee can possibly be the responsibility of either or both parents. However, the retainer form should very clearly indicate that the lawyer is representing the child and not the parents. This is most important, because often, in cases involving children, the claims of the parents and the children become polarized, and it should be clear from the outset that the lawyer is representing the child and not the parents, leaving the parents free to retain their own lawyer. As a practical matter, it is always more desirable for the lawyer representing the child, if being paid by the parents, to insist on a large retainer at the outset, to be placed in trust, allowing him to act according to the child's instructions and interests without being compromised by the parents' later refusal to pay.

As we have seen in Chapter 5, an alternative and more common method of payment in Ontario is through legal aid, a service available in every jurisdiction of the province. For obvious reasons, it is advisable for the lawyer to go with the child when he applies for legal aid, or to provide the child with a letter explaining that the child has come to his office in need of legal help, detailing the kind of legal services necessary, and estimating the eventual cost.

On attending, the child may be faced with the question of why his parents cannot or will not make the money available. In my experience, I have found that a difference of opinion and the refusal of the parents to provide for the cost of legal services is sufficient reason to grant the child an independent certificate, which will be sent directly to the lawyer already sought out by the child. It may take one to three weeks for the certificate to be processed. Where there is an emergency situation, and there is not enough time to make an application in this manner, a lawyer can usually telephone someone at a legal aid office in order to obtain an oral authorization for whatever emergency steps are necessary.

The Appendix provides an outline of children's resources which may prove useful in questioning a lawyer as to his knowledge of the subject and thus his approach to representing children. Without such knowledge, his ability to assist children and families is certainly limited and his approach will probably be narrowly legalistic. In the City of Toronto, for example, "the four-phase system" has been implemented to provide, in theory, a cohesive and continuous change of interrelated services which facilitate the movement of a child through distinct phases of treatment. The four phases are supposed to include:

Phase One: Overview, coordination, holding, assessment.

Phase Two: Short term treatment, psychiatric back-up.

Phase Three: Long term treatment, rural residence.

Phase Four: Reintegration into the urban community.

In Metropolitan Toronto there are various four-phase programs operating, restricted to various geographical catchment areas (east, west, and central Metro). Again, knowing about such programs helps to reduce the child's confusion when caught between the multitudinous bureaucracies.

The quality of treatment offered in the four-phase programs, however, can be variable, to say the least. "Birmingham Jail", the horror described at the beginning of Chapter 5 is part of a Phase Three residential facility. Or was. Fortunately, the place has now been torn down, and its unmourned passing should give us hope for the death of all our other institutions which use force against children, violate their cultural identity, deny or dilute their educational opportunities, or obscure their rights to proper legal counsel.

Our choices are quite simple, really. If we want tomorrow's Canadian society to be confused and hostile, suspicious of itself and the world, and lacking all direction, we are off to a good start in our present mistreatment of children. If we want something better, we will need to recognize the child as a citizen of our society, as a person worthy of respect and able to function as an enriched and enriching part of our civilization. If we fail with our "problem children" today, we can only reap the whirlwind in future; the "problems" are all too often our own; our children *are* the future.

FOOTNOTES

1 *R. v. Lewis* (1903), 7 C.C.C. 261, 6 O.L.R. 132
2 *Re K*, unreported decision of the Provincial Court (Family Division) Judicial District of Peel, March 1977
3 From the transcript of *E. v. E.* unreported decision, Supreme Court of Ontario, July 10th, 1979
4 *Re L.* (1962) 2 All English Reports 1
5 *Wakaluk v. Wakaluk* (1976) 25 R.F.L. 292 and 299 (Sask. C.A.)
6 *Re Tomyn*, unreported decision, Supreme Court of Ontario, June 16, 1977
7 *Re C*, unreported decision of the Provincial Court (Family Division) Judicial District of York, June 26th, 1979
8 *Children's Aid Society v. Reeves* (1975) 23 R.F.L. 391
9 The author acknowledges and thanks David Henry, social worker and director of Teen Family in Thunder Bay, for permitting an interview with him to be published in this fashion.
10 *Kilmar and Resney* (1973) 2 O.R. 482
11 *Re Squire* (1974) 16 R.F.L. 266
12 *McLeod v. Salmon Arm School Trustees* (1952) 2 D.L.R. 562 at 563
13 *Peter Mills v. Board of Education of the District of Columbia* (1973) 348 F. Supp. 866 at 876
14 See *Solicitor's Journal* 75, June 27th, 1933
15 *Campeau v. R.* (1951), 103 C.C.C. 355
16 *Daniels v. Evans* (1966) 224 A. (2nd) 63 at 64
17 *Walker v. Sheffield Brauns Powder Company Limited* (1977) 16 O.R. (2nd) 101 at 107
18 *LaPrairie v. LaPrairie* (1976) 29 R.F.L. 207

19 From the transcript of *Re K, supra*
20 From the transcript of *Re T.*, Provincial Court (Family Division) Judicial District of Peel, August 1977
21 *Re E.W.Z.* (1975) 23 R.F.L. 82
22 *Tabener v. Tabener* (1971) 5 R.F.L. 14
23 *Robson v. Robson* (1969) 2 O.R. 857 at 863
24 From the transcript of *Re K, supra*

SUGGESTED RELATED READINGS

CHAPTER ONE
Birkenmayer, A., Polonski, M., Beckett, J. and Ardron, D., *A Review of Alternatives to the Incarceration of the Youthful Offender*, Ontario Ministry of Corrections, 1976.
Cole, Amy, *Our Children's Keepers: Inside America's Kid Prisons* (New York: Grossman, 1972).
Kittrie, N., *The Right to be Different* (J. Hopkins Press, 1971).
Moyer, *The Pre-Judicial Exercise of Discretion and Its Impact on Children: A Review of the Literature* (Toronto: Centre for Criminology, University of Toronto, 1975).
Schur, *Radical Non-Intervention: Rethinking the Delinquency Problems* (Prentice-Hall 1973).

CHAPTER TWO
Brown, J., "Rootedness", in *Family Involvement Journal* (Toronto: Canadian Education Programs, May-June, 1974).
Family Involvement Journal, *Birthparents Tell their Stories* (Toronto, Canadian Education Programs, Volume Nine, Number Five, 1977).
Fisher, Florence, *The Search for Anna Fisher* (New York: Arthur Fields Book Inc., 1973).
Goldstein, J., Freud A., and Solnit, A.J., *Beyond the Best Interests of the Child* (New York: Free Press, 1973).
Goldstein, J., Freud A., and Solnit A.J., *Before the Best Interests of the Child* (New York: Free Press, 1979).
Mnookin, R.H., "Child Custody Adjudication: Judicial Functions in the Face of Indeterminancy", in *Children and the Law*, (1975), 39 *Law and Contemp. Probl. 226*.

Van Stolk, M., *The Battered Child in Canada* (Toronto: McClelland and Stewart, 1972).
Wald, M.S., "States Intervention on Behalf of 'Neglected' Children: A Search for Realistic Standards", (1975), 27 *Standford L. Rev. 625.*

CHAPTER THREE
Bargen, P.F., *The Legal Status of the Canadian Public School Pupil* (Toronto: Macmillan & Co., 1961).
Brooks, Ian R., "Native Education in Canada and the U.S.: A Bibliography" (Calgary: Indian Students University Program, Office of Educational Development, University of Calgary, 1976).
Coleman, James S., *et al., Equality of Education Opportunity* (Washington, D.C.: U.S. Department of Health, Education and Welfare, U.S. Government Printing Office, 1966).
Commission of Emotional and Learning Disorders in Children, *One Million Children* (Toronto: CELDIC, 1969).
Illich, I., *Deschooling Society*, 1971
Mosteller, F. and Moynihan, D. (eds.), *On Equality of Educational Opportunity* (New York: Random House, 1972).
Polk, K. and Schafer (eds.), *Schools and Delinquency* (New York: Prentice-Hall, 1972).

CHAPTER FOUR
British Columbia Law Reform Commission, *Report on Minor's Contracts*, Victoria, 1976.
Coleman, James S. *et al, Youth: Transition to Adulthood*, Report by the Panel on Youth of the President's Science Advisory Committee, Chicago: University of Chicago Press, 1974.
De Lone, R.H., For the Carnegie Council on Children, *Small Futures* (New York: Harcourt Brace Jovanovich, Inc. 1971).
Keniston, K. and the Carnegie Council on Children, *All Our Children: The American Family under Pressure* (New York: Harcourt Brace Jovanovich, Inc. 1977).
National Council on Welfare, "One in a World of Two's: A Report on One-Parent Families in Canada", Ottawa, 1976.

CHAPTER FIVE

Adams, Paul, Berg, Leila *et al, Children's Rights: Toward the Liberation of the Child,* Introduction by Paul Goodman (New York: Praeger Publishers, 1971).

Aries, Phillipe, *Centuries of Childhood* (New York: Alfred A. Knopf, 1962).

Canadian Council on Children and Youth, *Admission Restricted* (Canadian Council on Children and Youth, 1978).

Erikson, Erik, *Childhood and Society* (New York: Norton, 1964, 2nd ed.).

Harvard Educational Review, *The Rights of Children* (Cambridge, Mass.: Harvard Education Review, 1974).

Holt, J., *Escape from Childhood* (New York: E.P. Dutton, 1974).

Keniston, Kenneth, *Youth and Dissent: The Rise of the New Opposition* (New York: Harcourt Brace Jovanovich, 1971).

Mill, J.S., *On Liberty* (New York: Bobbs-Merrill Co. Inc., 1956).

Neill, A.S. *Summerhill* (New York: Hart Publishing Co., 1960).

CHAPTER SIX

Katz, S.N. (ed.), *The Youngest Minority: Parts I and II,* Lawyers in Defence of Children (American Bar Association, Section on Family Law, 1974).

Leeding, A.E., *Child Care Manual for Social Workers* (London: Butterworths, 1971).

Prudence, S., Naylor, A. and Patterson, J., *The Challenge of Daycare* (New Haven: Yale University Press, 1977).

Report, "The Medical Consent of Minors", British Columbia Royal Commission on Family and Children's Law, Report #12, Victoria, 1975.

Roocher, G.P. (ed.), *Children's Rights and the Mental Health Professions* (New York: Wiley, 1976).

Solnit, A.J., M.D., "Child-rearing and Child Advocacy", (1976) *Brigham Young University Law Review* 723-733

Wadlington, "Minors and Health Care: The Age of Consent", (1973), 11 *Osgoode Hall L.J. 115.*

A RESOURCE LIST OF SELECTED CHILDREN'S SERVICES ACROSS CANADA

National

Canadian Council of Children and Youth
322 Chapel Street
Ottawa, Ontario K1N 7Z2
613-924-8363

Canadian Human Rights Foundation
1980 Sherbrooke Street West, Suite 340
Montreal, Quebec H3H 1E8
514-932-7826

Canadian Mental Health Association (mental health/Canada)
National Office, 2160 Yonge Street
Toronto, Ontario M4S 2Z3
416-484-7750

Canadian Society for the Prevention of Cruelty to Children
Box 700
Midland, Ontario L4R 4P4
705-526-5647

Christian Children's Fund of Canada
1407 Yonge Street
Toronto, Ontario M4T 1Y8
416-922-2767

Council on Drug Abuse
56 The Esplanade East, Suite 303
Toronto, Ontario M5E 1A7
416-367-0183

Foster Parent's Plan of Canada
153 St. Clair Avenue West
Toronto, Ontario M4V 1P8
416-920-1654

Justice for Children
(The Canadian Foundation for Children and the Law Inc.)
455 Spadina Avenue, Suite 215
Toronto, Ontario

Planned Parenthood Federation of Canada
1226A Wellington St.
Ottawa, Ontario K1Y 3A1
613-722-3484 (provincial offices listed under each province)

United Jewish Appeal of Canada Inc.
1310 Greene Avenue
Montreal, Quebec H3Z 2B2
514-932-1431
   or
305-10182 103 Street
Edmonton, Alberta T5J 0Y5
403-429-1287

Provincial

Alberta

Alberta Council on Child and Family Welfare
11 Laxton Place, S.W.
Calgary, Alberta T3E 5E7

Alberta Human Rights and Civil Liberties Association
10348-96 St.
Edmonton, Alberta
403-424-4106

Birth Control Association (Calgary)
223-12th Avenue S.W.,
Calgary, Alberta T2R 0G9
403-261-9821

Calgary Family Service Bureau
120 13th Avenue S.E.
P.O. Box 2100
Calgary, Alberta T2G 2M5

Family Counselling Services
5000 Bowness Road, N.W.
Calgary, Alberta T3B 0B9
   or
912 McLeod Building
Edmonton, Alberta

Family Services Association of Edmonton
9919 106th Street
Edmonton, Alberta T5K 1E2
403-424-4161

Jewish Family Services
10136-100 St., Room 606
Edmonton, Alberta T5J 0P1
403-424-6346

Legal Aid Alberta
401, Melton Building
10310 Jasper Avenue
Edmonton, Alberta T5J 2W4

Legal Aid Alberta South
Main Floor, Rocky Mountain Plaza, 100
615 MacLeod Trail S.E.
Calgary, Alberta T2G 4T8

Planned Parenthood Alberta
100-233 12th Avenue S.W.
Calgary, Alberta T2R 0G9

Planned Parenthood Edmonton
308 McLeod Building
10136-100 Street
Edmonton, Alberta T5J 0P1

British Columbia

B.C. Civil Liberties Association
203-207 West Hastings
Vancouver, B.C. V6B 1H7

B.C. Human Rights Council
1254 West 7th Avenue
Vancouver, B.C. V6B 1B6

City of Vancouver Health Department
453 West 12th Avenue
Vancouver, B.C. V5Y 1V4

Crisis Intervention and Public Information Society of Victoria
1290 Gladstone, Box 5112, Station B
Victoria, B.C. V8R 6N3
604-386-6328

Crisis Intervention and Suicide Prevention Centre for Greater Vancouver
1946 West Broadway
Vancouver, B.C. V6J 1Z2

Family Services of Greater Vancouver
1616 West 7th Avenue
Vancouver, B.C. B6J 1S5

Jewish Family Service Agency
950 41st Avenue West
Vancouver, B.C. V5Z 2N7
604-266-2396

Lawyer Referral Service
202-1148 Hornby Street
Vancouver, B.C. 6Z2 2C3

Legal Aid Society of British Columbia
195 Alexander St.
Vancouver, B.C. V6A 1N3

Planned Parenthood B.C.
96 E. Broadway, Ste. 101
Vancouver, B.C. V5T 1V6

Social Services Dept.
Vancouver General Hospital
855 West 12th Avenue
Vancouver, B.C. V5Z 1M9

Manitoba

Alcohol and Drug Education Service
107-109 Christie Building
249½ Notre Dame Ave.
Winnipeg, Man.
204-942-2907

Children's Aid Society of Winnipeg
123-b Marion Street
Winnipeg, Man. R2H 0T3
   or
4-114 Garry Street
Winnipeg, Man. R3C 1G3
204-942-0511

Children's Home of Winnipeg
1712 Lorette Avenue
Winnipeg, R3M 1V8
204-452-9330

Family Services of Winnipeg, Inc.
254 Edmonton Street
Winnipeg, Man. R3C 1R9
204-947-1401

Health Dept., City of Winnipeg
4th floor, Admin. Building
Civic Centre
Winnipeg, Man. R3B 1B9

Jewish Child and Family Service
3rd floor, 956 Main
Winnipeg, Man. R2W 3P4
204-589-6343

Legal Aid Services Society
325 Portage Ave.
Winnipeg, Man. R3V 2C1

Manitoba Human Rights Commission
200-323 Portage Avenue
Winnipeg, Man. R3B 2C1

Manitoba Office of the Ombudsman
509-491 Portage Ave.
Winnipeg, Man. R3B 2E4

Planned Parenthood Manitoba
304-504 Main
Winnipeg, Man. R3B 1B8
204-943-6489

New Brunswick

Comité des Droits de l'Homme du Nord-Est du N.B.
Edifice Municipal
Lameque, N.B. E0B 1V0
506-344-2216

Family Planning Association of Fredericton
749 Charlotte St.
Fredericton, N.B. E3B 1M6

Family Services, St. John
5 Wall St.
St. John, N.B. E2K 3W3

Legal Aid, New Brunswick
358 King St., P.O. Box 1144
Fredericton, N.B.

New Brunswick Civil Liberties Association
7 Laurier Drive
Oromocto, N.B.
506-357-6847

Office of the Ombudsman
P.O. Box 6000
703 Brunswick Street
Fredericton, N.B. E3B 5H1

Planned Parenthood New Brunswick
Victoria Health Centre
43 Brunswick St.
Fredericton, N.B. E3B 1G5
506-454-1808

Newfoundland and Labrador

Community Services Council
Ft. William Building, P.O. Box 5116
St. John's, Nfld. A1C 1E8

Nfld.-Labrador Human Rights Association
Box 6182, St. John's, A1C 5X8
709-754-0690

Nfld. Legal Aid Commission
Centre Building, 4th floor
St. John's A0C 3Z8

Labrador Legal Services
38 Grenfell St., P.O. Box 899
Happy Valley, Labrador A0P 1E0

The Parliamentary Commission (Ombudsman)
Prudential Building,
49-55 Elizabeth Avenue
St. John's A1C 5T7

Planned Parenthood Nfld. and Labrador
Ft. William Building
21 Factory Lane
St. John's A1C 3J8
709-753-7333

Northwest Territories and Yukon Territory

Dept. of Child Welfare and Human Resources
Box 2703
Whitehorse, YT Y1A 2C6

Dept. of National Health and Welfare, Yukon Region
2 Hospital Road
Whitehorse, YT Y1A 3H8

Dept. of Social Services
Family and Children's Services
P.O. Box 1320
Yellowknife, N.W.T.

Health Care Division
Dept. of Social Services
Yellowknife, N.W.T.

Yukon Dept. of Justice
P.O. Box 2703
Whitehorse, YT Y1A 2C6

Yukon Family Services Assoc.
503 Cook St.
Whitehorse, YT Y1A 2R3
403-873-6112

Yukon Planned Parenthood
c/o Yukon Family Services
4078 4th Ave., Ste. 5
Whitehorse, YT Y1A 4K8
403-667-2970

Nova Scotia

Children's Aid Society of Halifax
5236 South St., P.O. Box 65
Halifax, N.S. B3J 2L4

Halifax Social Services
5450 Cornwallis St.
Halifax, N.S. B3K 1A9

Nova Scotia Legal Aid
5212 Sackville St., Suite 301
Halifax, N.S.

Office of the Ombudsman
P.O. Box 2152, Royal Bank Building
Halifax, B3J 3B7

Planned Parenthood Nova Scotia
1815 Hollis Street
Halifax, N.S. B3J 1W3
902-423-2090

Ontario

Addiction Research Foundation
33 Russell St.
Toronto, Ont.
416-595-6000

Catholic Children's Aid Society of Metropolitan Toronto
26 Maitland St.
Toronto, Ont. M4Y 1C6
416-925-6641

Children's Aid Society of Toronto
33 Charles St. E.
Toronto, Ont. M4Y 1R9
416-924-4646

Children's Aid Society, Ottawa
1370 Banks St.
Ottawa, Ont. K1H 7Y3
613-733-0670

Family Services Association of Metropolitan Toronto
22 Wellesley St. E.
Toronto, Ont. M4Y 1G3
416-922-3126

Family Services Centre of Ottawa
119 Ross Ave.,
Ottawa, Ont. K1Y 0N6

Jewish Family and Child Services of Metropolitan Toronto
3101 Bathurst St., 5th floor
Toronto, Ont. M6A 2A6
416-781-7592

League for Human Rights
825 Eglinton Ave. W.
Toronto, Ont. M5N 1E7
416-787-1259

Ontario Association of Children's Aid Societies
663 Yonge St.
Toronto, Ont. M4Y 2A4
416-924-2094

Ontario Legal Aid Plan
145 King St. W., Ste. 1000
Toronto, Ont. M5M 3L7
416-361-0766

Ontario Human Rights Commission
400 University Avenue, 12th floor
Toronto, Ont. M7A 1T7
416-965-6841

Parent Finders Inc.
28 York Valley Cres.
Willowdale, Ont. M4T 1M9
416-964-0794

Planned Parenthood Toronto
63 Yorkville Ave.
Toronto, Ont. M5R 1B7
416-961-8290

V.D. Hotline
416-965-3333

Prince Edward Island

Catholic Family Services Bureau
P.O. Box 698
Charlottetown, P.E.I. C1A 7L3

Office of the Public Defender
193 Grafton St., P.O. Box 205
Charlottetown C1A 7K4

P.E.I. Civil Liberties Association
Box 1834, 202 Grafton St.
Charlottetown
902-894-9260

Planned Parenthood P.E.I.
1-76B Kent St.
Charlottetown C1A 4B6
902-892-8141

Protestant Family Service Bureau
216 Queen St. P.O. Box 592
Charlottetown, C1A 7L1

Quebec

Centre communautaire juridique de Québec
175, boul. Benoit XV, App. 1
Québec, Québec G1L 2Y8

Centre de Services Sociaux de Québec
999, de Bourgagne
Ste.-Foy, Québec G1W 4S6

La Fédération du Québec pour le planning des naissances
3826 rue St. Hubert
Montréal, Québec
514-842-9501

La Ligue des Droits de L'Homme
3836 rue St. Hubert
Montréal, Québec H2L 4A5
514-844-2815

Jewish Community Council of Montreal
5491 Victoria Ave.
Montréal, Québec H3W 2P9
514-739-6363

Planned Parenthood Association, Montréal
336 est, rue Sherbrooke
Montréal, Québec H2X 1E6

Saskatchewan

Association on Human Rights, Regina
2067 Roe St.
Regina, Sask.
306-584-4816

Association on Human Rights, Saskatoon
311-20th St. W.
Saskatoon, Sask. S7M 0X1

Community Legal Services Commission
3130 8th St. E.
Saskatoon, Sask. S7K 0B7

Family Services Bureau of Regina
1801 Toronto St.
Regina, Sask. S4P 1M7

Planned Parenthood Saskatchewan
404-245 Third Avenue S.
Saskatoon, Sask. S7K 1M4
306-664-2050

Saskatchewan Human Rights Commission
219-A-2 1st St. E.
Saskatoon, Sask. S7K 0B7

Saskatoon Family Service Bureau
20, 309-22nd St. E.
Saskatoon, Sask. S7K 0G7

Native People

B.C. Native Women's Society
P.O. Box 27
Kamloops, B.C.
804-374-9412

Calgary Indian Friendship Centre
140-2 Avenue S.W.
Calgary, Alta. T2P 0B9
403-264-1155

Calgary Urban Indian Youth
c/o Room 306, 223-12th Ave. S.W.
Calgary, Alta. T2R 0G9
403-265-4728

Federation of Saskatchewan Indians
1114 Central Ave., P.O. Box 1644
Prince Albert, Sask.
306-764-3411

Indian Association of Alberta
203-11710 Kingsway Ave.
Edmonton, Alta. T5G 0X5
403-452-7221

Manitoba Indian Brotherhood
500-275 Portage Avenue
Winnipeg, Man. R3B 2B3
204-944-8245

National Association of Friendship Centres
200 Cooper St., Suite 2
Ottawa, Ont. K2P 0G1
613-232-1761

National Indian Brotherhood
102 Bank St., 1st floor
Ottawa, Ont. K1P 5N4
613-236-0673

Native Association of Nfld. and Labrador
Box 1195
St. John's, Nfld.

Native Canadian Centre of Toronto
16 Spadina Road
Toronto, Ont. M5R 2S8
416-964-9087

Native Youth Association of Canada
c/o 130 Alberta Street, 6th floor
Ottawa, Ont.
613-238-3511

Special Education

Alberta Assoc. for Children with Learning Disabilities
10180-108 St. Ste 201
Edmonton, Alberta T5J 1L3
403-426-5965

Association for Bright Children
c/o University of Toronto Schools
371 Bloor St. W.
Toronto M5S 2R8
416-222-7256

Canadian Association for Children with Learning Disabilities
Kildare House
323 Chapel St.
Ottawa K1N 7Z2
613-238-5721

Manitoba Assoc. for Children with Learning Disabilities
Room 5, 1070 Clifton St.
Winnipeg, Man. R3E 2T7
204-775-3919

Ontario Assoc. for Children with Learning Disabilities
60 St. Clair Ave. E., Suite 202
Toronto M4T 1N5
416-961-8524

Ontario Association of Alternative and Independent Schools
3199 Bathurst St., Toronto M6A 2B2
416-781-7633

Quebec Assoc. for Children with Learning Disabilities
4820 Van Horne Ave., Suite 8
Montreal M3W 1J3
514-735-1636

Sask. Assoc. for Children with Learning Disabilities
Room 7, Herchmer School
1132 McTavish St.
Regina, Sask. S4T 3V5

Sex Information and Education Council of Canada
423 Castlefield Avenue, Toronto M5N 1Z2
416-483-8805

Society for Indian and Northern Education
College of Education
University of Saskatchewan
Saskatoon, Sask. S7N 0W0

Canadian Association Of Law Guardians

Public Trustee,
Attorney General's Dept.
Madison Bldg,
9919 105th St.
Edmonton, Alberta
T5K 2E8
Tel. 403-427-5684

Public Trustee,
Attorney General's Ministry,
625 Burrard St.,
Vancouver, B.C.
Tel: 604-685-2431

Public Trustee,
Dept. of Attorney General
7th Floor, Woodsworth Bldg.,
405 Broadway Avenue
Winnipeg, Man.
R3C 3L6
Tel: 204-944-2703

Department of Health,
Dept. of Social Services,
Fredericton, New Brunswick

Department of Justice
Centennial Bldg.,
Fredericton, N.B.
E3B 5H1

Public Trustee,
The Anchorage House, Ste. 159
Historic Properties,
Halifax, Nova Scotia
B3J 1F9
Tel: 902-424-7760

Official Guardian of Ontario
Attorney General's Ministry
180 Dundas St. West,
Toronto, Ont. M5G 1E4
Tel: 416-965-1865

Office of the Public Curator,
Stock Exchange Tower,
Box 51,
Montreal, Quebec
H4Z 1J6
Tel: 514-873-4074

Official Guardian
Saskatchewan Attorney General
City Hall,
2476 Victoria Avenue,
Regina, Saskatchewan
S4P 3V7
Tel: 306-565-5440

Research Director,
Law Reform Commission,
1003-201st St. E.
Saskatoon, Saskatchewan

Public Administrator and
Official Guardian,
Whitehorse,
Yukon Territory

INDEX